WINTER DRINKS

WINTER DRINKS

70 Essential Cold-Weather Cocktails

the Editors of PUNCH

photography by
Lizzie Munro

TEN SPEED PRESS
California | New York

CONTENTS

COCKTAIL LIST

What exactly defines a winter drink? When we look through the history of cocktails, there are a number of drinks that have become synonymous with a season: no one would argue against the daiquiri, the piña colada, the margarita, or, of late, the spritz as being the cocktail-world equivalents of a "Greetings from Paradise" postcard. Likewise, when that first hint of winter comes marching in, there are drinks that have historically been its flag bearers.

Hot toddy. Mulled wine. Spiked cider. Hot buttered rum. Irish coffee. The cocktail world's classic hot drinks have long led that procession—they are, after all, drinks quite literally built to fortify us against the cold. But winter drinking today goes far beyond spiking one's mug of steaming liquid with rum or whiskey. The craft cocktail renaissance has cracked open a brave new world of possibilities. Today, a "winter drink" can span everything from herbal coolers to batched and bottled cocktails for a crowd to concoctions like the daiquiri—whose all-important citrus component is, it should be noted, at its prime in winter—reimagined with cool weather in mind.

So, where to start? Many of the drinks that home enthusiasts call on for their winter menus are mere tweaks and riffs on existing classic cocktail blueprints. That's why our exploration of what winter drinking means today begins with the ten essential classic cocktails that feel best suited to winter—think the Manhattan, champagne cocktail, old-fashioned, and more. As everyone from the Dalai Lama to Social Distortion has said: Learn the rules before you break them. In cocktails, the same is true. Once you understand the most basic cocktail blueprints, it becomes easy to bend them in order to make them your own.

To that end, there are just as many best practices as there are hacks and shortcuts in this book. You'll learn the ins and outs of making a spirit infusion; how to batch drinks for a crowd; how to bottle your favorite stirred drinks and freeze them ahead for on-the-fly Manhattans and martinis; three-step syrups and shrubs to keep on hand; and the tips and tools you'll need to build a winter-ready bar. You'll also learn how to turn everything from a piña colada to a margarita into drinks that feel more at home in a fireside armchair than a beachside lounger. (*Believe in the winter piña colada.*)

This collection of seventy recipes is packed with hot, spiced, and buttered seasonal imperatives, plus plenty of our editors' nostalgic favorites and homegrown creations. Our aim, beyond fortifying you against the cold and arming you for the holidays, is to take the best of what we at PUNCH are seeing from today's top bartenders and make it accessible for home bartenders—because, after all, that's exactly what we are.

ANATOMY
OF A
WINTER
COCKTAIL

What is a nog, *really*? Questions featuring this kind of existential prodding are of great concern to us at PUNCH. You are what you drink, after all. Although it's not absolutely crucial to understand the ins and outs of every cocktail in history to whip up a winter drink, it's a useful starting point if you aim to get creative on your own. So, first things first: know your nogs from your glöggs and your sours from your smashes. Here's a quick guide to the main cocktail families and their more esoteric winter brethren.

CLASSIC COCKTAIL FAMILIES

Most of the cocktail canon's classic and modern drinks fit into these ten categories.

Cocktail

While the word *cocktail* has become synonymous with "mixed drink," it actually refers to a *style* of drink: a simple combination of spirit, sweetener (generally sugar or sugar syrup), water, and bitters. The old-fashioned is the archetype. Today, we also use this category to refer to the drinks that rely on this formula with the addition of either vermouth or liqueurs—think Manhattan, martini, and Negroni.

Sour

These are drinks made with a base spirit, fresh citrus, and a sweetener (again, generally sugar or a sugar syrup). The most classic example is the daiquiri. A subcategory of the sour is the daisy, which refers to the same formula but with a liqueur (or grenadine) in place of, or in addition to, sugar or sugar syrup. The margarita and the sidecar are the icons of this subcategory.

Collins

Your classic collins is basically a sour lengthened with the addition of sparkling water. In this category, no drink looms larger than the Tom Collins, which is a combination of gin, lemon juice, simple syrup, and soda water (i.e., boozy, bubbly lemonade). The collins even has its own namesake glass.

Highball

The highball is a more stripped-down collins. Simply a combination of spirit plus a larger proportion of nonalcoholic mixer, the highball likewise has its own glass, which is a slightly larger, by volume, version of the collins glass. Drinks like the whiskey-ginger, Jack-and-Coke, and scotch-and-soda all fall under the highball umbrella.

Fizz

The fizz is essentially a sour made tall by adding soda water—which, of course, sounds exactly like a collins. There's a debate among cocktail authorities as to how fizzes differ from collins drinks, but there is some consensus that fizzes are shaken and strained, while a collins is built in the glass and stirred. Another difference: fizzes commonly allow the addition of egg white and/or cream (think Ramos gin fizz). In fact, when referring to a fizz drink today, it is often implied that the drink will include one or both additions.

Punch

Punch is not the only drink category to be known primarily by its serveware, but it is certainly the most famous. The "flowing bowl," as it were, does in fact have a definition, though it has shape-shifted over the course of its history of nearly four hundred years. Originally it was defined by four or five central ingredients: spirit, citrus, water, sweetener, and, often, spice. That eventually evolved to include the addition of wines like sherry, port, and champagne—sometimes all of the above in a single bowl. Today the formula has, like all classic formulas, been updated and refashioned to suit the needs of many a ladle-wielding host.

Cobbler

An offshoot of the punch family tree, a cobbler is, at its most basic, a mix of a spirit or fortified wine, sugar, and fruit, served over crushed ice with a straw. The category is thought to have originated in early nineteenth-century America with the advent of readily available ice. Once considered the height of fashion, the drink largely fell out of favor until the recent cocktail revival. The sherry cobbler remains the category's primary ambassador, though today you will find cobblers that call on everything from mezcal to amaro.

Julep | Smash

The julep and the smash are both defined by a combination of base spirit, sweetener, crushed ice, and generally lots of mint. Both are among the oldest American cocktail types. Traditionally, the smash was a diminutive julep—meant to be thrown back rather than savored—and was, over the years, rolled under the julep umbrella. Of late, it has roared back to reclaim its place as a drink that is separate, if ill-defined, by modern terms. Today, a smash is often a mixture of a base spirit, sweetener, and muddled mint and citrus, shaken together and served over ice.

Buck | Mule

This family of drinks distinguishes itself by the addition of ginger ale or ginger beer to a base of spirit and citrus, served over ice. The most famous examples of this category is the Moscow Mule, a relatively late addition with an invention date in the 1950s, and the Dark 'n' Stormy, a simple combination of dark rum, lime, and ginger beer.

Sling

A precursor to the original cocktail, the slings of the eighteenth century were nearly interchangeable with the toddy and could be served either hot or cold. By the mid-1800s, the sling was more commonly served cold and the toddy served hot. Add bitters to this formula and *voilà*—you've got the original cocktail, the old-fashioned. (A funny historical side note: the most famous drink to bear the sling name, the Singapore sling, is not technically a sling, but a tikified punch.)

CLASSIC WINTER FORMULAS

These drinks and drink types are commonly associated with cold-weather drinking.

Bishop

While the bishop essentially falls under the umbrella of punch, its immortalization in literature (namely, in Dickens' *A Christmas Carol*) as a symbol of redemption and holiday cheer has helped carve it a niche all its own. A hot drink based on port wine and infused with everything from ginger to cloves to orange peels, the bishop has existed since at least 1755.

Flip | Nog

While egg whites might show up in sours or fizzes, any drink with a whole egg could be considered a flip, a category that has been floating around since the seventeenth century. The modern version usually works like this: a base spirit, a whole egg, and a sweetener, shaken and served with grated nutmeg. While the flip diminished in popularity, eggnog (which dates back to the eighteenth century) became the one drink to carry forth the tradition of blending eggs and booze across multiple generations. Another Christmastime classic, the Tom and Jerry, has also endured as one of this category's ambassadors.

Hot Buttered Rum, Whiskey, and More

Plopping butter into booze has been going on, according to cocktail historian David Wondrich, since at least the days of Henry VIII. While the practice began with the addition of butter to beer, it's theorized that butter first met spirit sometime during the eighteenth century. It endures today as an archaic, but still much-loved holiday drink built on a base of rum, though scotch or bourbon are also intermittent companions.

Mulled Cider, Wine, and More

The process of mulling a beverage simply refers to infusing it with spices—typically a mixture of cinnamon, cloves, allspice, and nutmeg—

and then heating the mixture. Long synonymous with the holiday season, mulled wine (the most common mulled beverage) dates back to the Roman era and, today, goes by many different monikers (*vin chaud* in France; *Glühwein* in Germany; and so on) and variations. The most famous variation is the Nordic *glögg*, which often calls on the addition of aquavit and additional spices, such as cardamom.

Toddy

Though the modern definition of the toddy almost always compromises any alcoholic beverage served hot, it wasn't always so. One of the ancestral drinks of the cocktail world, the toddy's origins likely came from a number of traditions, but it loosely meant a base spirit (usually rum or whiskey) plus a sweetener and water, served either hot or cold. Today the usage generally refers to a hot drink that includes a base spirit plus sweetener, hot water, citrus, and spices (clove and cinnamon, typically), though more complex iterations abound.

Wassail

Wassail is both an old English toast to one's health (wassail!) and a large-format hot drink that can be made from a base of wine (dry red wine or sherry are typical), beer, or cider that's infused with spices, a sweetener, and baked apples. There are countless variations on the formula.

While most of these drink types and families refer to blueprints for single-serve drinks, nearly every recipe in the history books can be scaled up to meet the demands of holiday revelry. All you need is a punch bowl or a pitcher and a few pro tips.

BATCHING FOR A CROWD

Practical logic would have the home bartender believe that if you want to make, say, four cocktails instead of one, you'd just multiply the recipe by four. But scaling up a recipe isn't simply a matter of doubling, tripling, or quadrupling each component.

The Rules of Batching

Here are a few hard-and-fast rules worth keeping in mind when approaching batched cocktails and large-format drinks at home.

KNOW YOUR RATIOS Most classic and more minimalist modern drinks break out into clean ratios (2-to-1-to-1, 1-to-1-to-1, 3-to-1, 2-to-1). Instead of multiplying ounces and then converting them to cups, it's often easier to start with the recipe's ratio and then adjust to taste. So, for example, to batch a classic Manhattan, instead of 2 ounces of whiskey to 1 ounce of vermouth, up it to 2 cups whiskey to 1 cup vermouth and then add bitters to taste.

START WITH THE GREATEST-VOLUME INGREDIENT The ingredients of the least volume, such as citrus, sweetener, and bitters, often have the largest margin for error. Start with the greatest-volume, nonaromatic ingredient, like the spirit base, and work up to the lesser-volume components, tasting as you go along.

SCALE BACK BITTERS OR OTHER AROMATIC INGREDIENTS When combined with alcohol, aromatic elements are amplified. As a rule of thumb, when adding ingredients like bitters or ginger syrup, add about half of what a batch appears to call for, and work up from there.

DON'T FORGET ABOUT DILUTION You can choose to dilute your batched cocktail or serve it over ice. A half ounce of water per serving is a good measurement to lean on. If you're working with a higher-octane cocktail like a martini or a Manhattan, you can up the dilution to one ounce per serving. Alternatively, you can forgo dilution in the batched drink and simply pour the cocktail over ice when ready to serve.

ADJUST TO TASTE Batching is as much adjusting the drink to your palate to achieve balance as it is about about minding your math. Bartender Leo Robitschek of New York's NoMad Bar aptly likens batching a drink to seasoning a dish as you cook it until you achieve the right balance of flavors.

Bottling and Freezing Cocktails

The process of batching and then freezing drinks like the martini and Manhattan has become a standard affair at bars around the country—and, subsequently, at PUNCH. There are obvious benefits, like the ability to pour martinis on demand, no stirring required, and standardizing how each drink tastes. But the less obvious side effect: freezing boozy cocktails ahead imparts a lush, creamy texture and polishes off some of the rough edges on bold ingredients like amaro and the "burn" one typically gets from classic stirred drinks that pull no punches. And, of course, it allows you more time with your guests. Here are a few things to consider when batching and freezing ahead at home.

What to Batch

Choose a stirred cocktail that is composed of a large quantity of spirit (two ounces or more). Think martini, Manhattan, or old-fashioned. For spirit-forward drinks that are slightly lower in proof overall, like the Negroni, you will need to slightly alter the ratio from 1-to-1-to-1 to 2-to-1-to-1, leaning on a larger quantity of gin to prevent the drink from freezing overnight.

How to Dilute

Stirred drinks contain anywhere from ½ to 1½ ounces of water per drink, depending on the length of stirring and type of ice that is used to stir them. We typically assume 1 ounce of filtered water per drink in our freeze-ahead recipes. Here are three tried-and-true ratios we use for bottling and freezing ahead.

MARTINI

3 parts gin

1 part dry vermouth

½ part water

MANHATTAN

4 parts whiskey, 100 proof or higher

2 parts sweet vermouth

¼ part Angostura bitters

1 part water

NEGRONI

2 parts gin

1 part Campari

1 part sweet vermouth

1 part water

WINTERIZING CLASSIC SUMMER DRINKS

It might seem counterintuitive to suggest that in a book built to showcase season-appropriate drinks, some drinks need not be relegated to a season. But it's true: with a few sleights of hand, summer classics like the daiquiri, margarita—even the piña colada—can be rebuilt to channel winter. In fact, they already have a leg up. The key component of many of summer's most iconic drinks—citrus—is actually most abundant in winter.

First things first: take stock of what's in season (see page 17) and what's not, and substitute as needed with ingredients at the peak of their ripeness in winter. For example, in the classic rum cooler the mojito—a combination of fresh herbs, sugar, citrus, rum, and soda water—it's easy to slot in alternative herbs and a richer spirit for an easy winter updo. In our Winter Mojito (page 69) we sub the rich, brooding blackstrap for white rum and replace mint with muddled rosemary. Same idea, different drink.

Another hot tip: when adjusting cocktails for a new season, the most forgiving to work with are long (i.e., "lengthened" with a nonalcoholic ingredient), bubbly drinks. In our cold-weather arsenal is a year-round PUNCH favorite, the spritz. Playing within the template of bitter, bubbly, and low alcohol offers a lot of options. First, consider swapping in richer bitter liqueurs, like amari, or aromatized wines, like spicy Barolo Chinato, and adding seasonal citrus, like blood orange, to the mix, as in our Sanguinello Spritz (page 82) or trading out prosecco for dry cider (see page 26), Lambrusco, or beer. Even drinks like the iconic summer cooler the Pimm's Cup are rife for winter riffing. In our winter version (see page 87) of the lavishly garnished British drink, we replace ginger ale with American lager and then crown the drink with a bounty of fresh winter herbs, apples, and cranberries for a head-turning holiday take on the classic.

When it comes to shaken drinks, like the gin sour or the daiquiri, syrups infused with seasonal herbs, spices, and fruits can dramatically change the flavor profile of a cocktail. Simply swap in a flavored syrup (see page 21) in place of regular simple syrup, and you've got just enough to give a classic drink a signature holiday look. Likewise, incorporating fresh herbs can go a long way. In our Winter Paloma (page 76), the addition of sage, both as an element in the drink and an aromatic garnish, takes it from the Mexican beachside to a drink evocative of winter. The gin and tonic, meanwhile, is winterized (see page 66) with the addition of an easy grapefruit shrub and muddled rosemary. Even the daiquiri is not immune to the winter treatment (see page 143).

Finally, there's that behemoth of summer drinking, the piña colada. How do you take a drink whose spirit relies on both a beach and a blender and make it the sort of thing you'd sip après ski? Turn it into a milk punch, of course. Our Piña Colada Milk Punch (page 125) maintains the drink's tropical spirit with coconut water, pineapple juice, and rum, but it's transformed by adding scalded milk, clarifying the mixture with a cheesecloth, and then ladling it, punch-style, on the rocks. And while it may sound complicated, it's actually a whole lot easier to batch and serve than your typical piña colada.

Some might even find these seasonal twists to be improvements on the classics; regardless, they make a strong case for not relegating any drink to one time of year. The paper umbrellas, though—that's your call.

STOCKING
YOUR
WINTER
BAR

While perusing the farmers' market in the dead of winter can be an exercise in deprivation—root vegetables, collard greens, more root vegetables—when it comes to drinks, winter offers a veritable bounty of fresh herbs and fruits that can be muddled, infused, or simply used as a means of aromatic complexity (and visual appeal). Of course, citrus—Persian and key lime, grapefruit, blood orange, lemon, and clementine—is also in season, but you know what to do there: muddle, juice, and garnish away.

WHAT'S IN SEASON AND HOW TO USE IT

Often the best place to look for winter inspiration is your local market. We often start with the fresh ingredient in a drink first, and then build on it by adding complementary flavors. Here are a few key ingredients at their zenith in fall and winter, and some tips on how to dispatch them in drinks.

APPLES One of our favorite applications for apples is in the Booze + Juice (page 84). Simply choose a variety that is tart by nature (think Granny Smith), juice it, and pair it with your spirit of choice over ice in a highball glass. Tangy, savory, and refreshing—it's the ultimate, no-fuss late-fall highball.

CONCORD GRAPES Concord grapes are prime for muddling into simple syrup and then shaking with gin and a bit of citrus; simply swap grapes for cranberries in our Cranberry Smash (page 55). They're also excellent candidates for a syrup (see page 21).

CONTINUED ON PAGE 20

A WORD ON SHRUBS

Born from an ancient Persian drink that dates back more than a thousand years, shrubs have come back into vogue as not only a cocktail ingredient, but also a way to preserve produce through the entirety of a season.

While early shrubs were simply a mix of citrus and sugar, kicked up with a spirit, today they are more commonly defined as a flavored syrup that is preserved with vinegar. It's essentially the drink world's *agrodolce* or *gastrique*—that is, a way to add tang and dimension to a cocktail. We tend to keep it simple when it comes to the shrub: add 1 ounce of any of the shrubs below to 2 ounces of spirit and then lengthen the mixture with soda water, sparkling wine, bubbly dry cider, or Lambrusco.

These recipes are three simple starting points, but really should be considered prompts more than end-points. Feel free to add fresh herbs, ginger, and additional spices to the mix for extra complexity.

CRANBERRY SHRUB

2 cups fresh or frozen cranberries

1½ cups pure cane sugar

1 cup water

3 cloves, crushed (optional)

½ to ¾ cup apple cider vinegar, preferably Bragg

Combine the cranberries, sugar, water, and cloves in a saucepan over medium-high heat. Let the mixture come to a boil, reduce the heat to low, and gently simmer until the cranberries begin to soften and break down, about 7 minutes. Let the mixture cool, then strain through a cheesecloth into a glass bottle or jar. Add the vinegar, scaling up to taste. Refrigerate for 24 hours before using. Store in the refrigerator for up to 6 months. MAKES ABOUT 2 CUPS

POMEGRANATE SHRUB

1½ cups pure cane sugar

Peels of 2 oranges

1 cup 100% pomegranate juice, such as POM Wonderful

½ to ¾ cup apple cider vinegar, preferably Bragg

In a mixing bowl, combine the sugar and the orange peels. Gently muddle the peels in the sugar to release their oils, then set aside for 20 minutes. In a saucepan, combine the sugar, peels, and pomegranate juice over very low heat and cook until the sugar has dissolved, about 5 minutes. Let the mixture cool before removing the peels and straining the mixture through a cheesecloth into a glass bottle or jar. Add the vinegar, scaling up to taste. Refrigerate for 24 hours before using. Store in the refrigerator for up to 6 months. MAKES ABOUT 2 CUPS

GRAPEFRUIT SHRUB

1½ cups pure cane sugar

Peels and ¾ cup juice from 1 ruby red grapefruit

1 teaspoon pink peppercorns, crushed (optional)

½ cup boiling water

½ to ¾ cup apple cider vinegar, preferably Bragg

In a mixing bowl, combine the sugar, grapefruit peels, and peppercorns. Gently muddle the peels in the sugar to release their oils, then set aside for 20 minutes. To the mixing bowl, add the boiling water and stir until the sugar has dissolved. Let the mixture cool before removing the peels. Add the juice and strain the mixture through a cheesecloth into a glass bottle or jar. Add the vinegar, scaling up to taste. Refrigerate for 24 hours before using. Store in the refrigerator for up to 6 months. MAKES ABOUT 2½ CUPS

CRANBERRIES The only logical thing to do when cranberries come into season is to make both a syrup (see page 21) and a shrub (see page 18). The latter can be made in large batches and kept all winter and into next season, maturing along the way. In syrup form, cranberries are the perfect substitute for simple syrup in just about any drink—whether it's a classic sour or a French 75 (page 45). We also like to muddle fresh or frozen cranberries for a tart, gin-based smash (see page 55).

LAVENDER It's quick and easy to macerate dried lavender in a London dry gin or vodka for a season-appropriate base. Same goes for lavender syrup; it's another great addition to the seasonal syrup arsenal.

MINT While many of the drinks that famously incorporate mint (mojito, southside, mint julep) all seem to channel warmer weather, mint is available fresh year-round and can add a bit of levity to richer drinks or an extra cooling element to citrus-forward cocktails. Incorporate it by muddling, garnishing, or both.

PEARS Crank up the oven, roast, and puree. Core and roast them at 375°F for 45 to 60 minutes, until soft. Let them cool, then puree. You can sweeten the puree with simple syrup (see page 23) or wait until you dispatch it in a drink to sweeten.

POMEGRANATES One word: grenadine, and not the sticky-sweet red stuff of Shirley Temples past. Using fresh pomegranate to make a grenadine syrup (see page 22) that can be swapped into drinks will not only give them color, but also the same sort of tartness that cranberry offers. They are also perfect for use in a vibrant shrub (see page 18).

ROSEMARY, THYME, SAGE The big three winter herbs can be incorporated as an infusion (see page 32), in a syrup (see page 21), as an aromatic garnish, or all of the above.

EASY SEASONAL SYRUPS

During the winter months, keep a few simple flavored syrups on hand as a foolproof way to whip up a house cocktail on the fly that feels bespoke for guests. Swap in any of these syrups for a recipe that calls for simple syrup, which is also included below. Just be sure to think about the existing flavors in a drink and choose a syrup that falls within the same flavor matrix.

CINNAMON SYRUP

3 cinnamon sticks, broken up   1 cup sugar
1 cup water

Combine the cinnamon sticks and water in a saucepan and bring to a boil over medium heat. Reduce the heat to low, add the sugar, and stir until the sugar dissolves, about 1 minute. Remove the pan from the heat and let the mixture cool and macerate for 1 hour. Strain through a cheesecloth into a glass bottle or jar and store in the fridge for up to 1 month. MAKES 1½ CUPS

CONCORD GRAPE SYRUP

2 cups Concord grapes   1 cup water
1 cup sugar

Combine grapes, sugar, and water in a saucepan over low heat. Gently crush the grapes as they soften, and stir until the sugar dissolves, about 5 minutes. Remove from the heat and set aside to cool and macerate for 30 minutes. Strain through cheesecloth into a glass jar and store in the fridge for up to 1 month. MAKES 1½ CUPS

CRANBERRY SYRUP

1½ cups fresh or
frozen cranberries

1 cup sugar

1 cinnamon stick,
crushed (optional)

1 cup water

Combine the cranberries, sugar, cinnamon, and water in a saucepan
over medium-high heat. Let the mixture come to a boil, reduce the heat
to low, and gently simmer until the cranberries begin to break down,
about 7 minutes. Let the mixture cool and macerate for 30 minutes.
Strain through cheesecloth into a glass jar and store in the fridge for
up to 1 month. MAKES 1½ CUPS

GINGER SYRUP

2 cups sugar

1 cup fresh ginger juice

Combine the sugar and ginger juice in a saucepan over low heat. Stir
until the sugar dissolves, about 5 minutes. Remove the pan from the
heat and let the mixture cool. Pour into a glass jar and store in the fridge
for up to 1 month. MAKES 1½ CUPS

GRENADINE

1½ cups 100% pomegranate
juice, preferably POM Wonderful

1 cup sugar

Pinch of salt

Peel of 1 orange

Bring 1 cup of the pomegranate juice to a boil in a saucepan over
medium heat, then lower the heat and simmer until the volume is
reduced by half, about 10 minutes. Add the remaining ½ cup pomegranate
juice and the sugar to the pan and continue to simmer, stirring, until
the sugar dissolves, about 3 minutes more. Remove the pan from the
heat and add the salt and orange peel, expressing the peel (twisting to
release the oils) into the liquid before adding the whole pieces. Let cool
completely, then strain through cheesecloth into a glass jar and store
in the fridge for up to 2 weeks. MAKES 1½ CUPS

HONEY SYRUP

1 cup honey   1 cup hot water

Combine the honey and hot water in a heat-safe jar and stir to combine, about 1 minute. Store in the fridge for up to 1 month. MAKES 1½ CUPS

LAVENDER SYRUP

1 tablespoon dried lavender buds   1 cup sugar
1 cup water

Combine the lavender buds and water in a saucepan and bring to a boil over medium heat. Reduce the heat to low, add the sugar, and stir until the sugar dissolves, about 1 minute. Remove the pan from the heat and let the mixture cool and macerate for 1 hour. Strain through cheesecloth into a glass jar and store in the fridge for up to 1 month. MAKES 1½ CUPS

SIMPLE SYRUP

1 cup cane sugar   1 cup water

Combine the sugar and water in a saucepan over low heat. Stir until the sugar dissolves, about 5 minutes. Remove from the heat and let the mixture cool. Store in a glass jar in the fridge for up to 1 month. MAKES 1½ CUPS

VANILLA SYRUP

1 cup sugar   1 vanilla bean
1 cup water

Combine the sugar and water in a saucepan over low heat. Split open the vanilla bean with a small knife and scrape the contents into the pan; add the bean pod. Stir until the sugar dissolves, about 5 minutes. Remove the pan from the heat and let the mixture cool and macerate for 1 hour. Strain through cheesecloth into a glass jar and store in the fridge for up to 1 month. MAKES 1½ CUPS

WINTER HERB SYRUP

2 large sprigs rosemary

2 bunches thyme

5 sage leaves

1 cup sugar

1 cup water

Wash the herbs and set them aside to dry. Combine the sugar and water in a saucepan over low heat. Add the herbs and stir until the sugar dissolves, about 3 minutes. Remove the pan from the heat and let the mixture cool and macerate for 1 hour. Strain through a cheesecloth into a glass jar and store in the fridge for up to 1 month. MAKES 1½ CUPS

USEFUL PANTRY ITEMS

While leaning on fresh produce is paramount when building drinks at home, pantry items you might normally stock for cooking and baking can also be transformed into cocktail ingredients. A pinch of this, a drop of that—when it comes to the items below, a little can go a long way.

CAYENNE A few of us on the PUNCH team are fond of adding a bit of a spicy kick to some of the syrups we keep on hand. Consider adding a scant ⅛ teaspoon (add it gradually, to taste) to a honey syrup, or mix it into a small container of maple syrup. It adds an extra dimension to any hot drink. Bonus: cayenne, which is part of the capsicum family, has a number of health benefits, including detox support.

CINNAMON A critical holiday flavor conduit, cinnamon sticks can be employed as an aromatic garnish (and stir stick) or grated over the top of a drink to add complexity. And, of course, we always recommend keeping a cinnamon syrup (see page 21) on hand.

MAPLE SYRUP Substituting pure maple syrup for simple syrup can add depth and richness to a drink, as in Erik Adkins's Filibuster (page 56), a play on the whiskey sour, or Erick Castro's breakfast-ready French Toast Flip (page 137). Be sure to mind sweetness when swapping in maple syrup by starting with a smaller amount (½ ounce instead of ¾ ounce, for example) and then scale up from there if needed.

NUTMEG For hundreds of years (in fact, since before the invention of the American "cocktail"), nutmeg has been a crucial cool-weather drink companion. An essential ingredient in punches, flips, toddies, and the like, it's an easy way to add a bit of holiday flair to a drink. It's primarily used as an aromatic ingredient, finely grated over a bowl of hot or cold punch or whole egg or egg-white drinks.

TEA In the recipes that follow, tea plays in an important role in punch-style drinks and hot drinks. It can also be swapped in for water in simple syrup to create a spiced tea syrup (see page 88) that can play nice with a number of cocktails. We always have black tea and Earl Grey on hand, as well as spiced teas, particularly chai, hibiscus, and holiday spice, the latter of which plays a role in our house favorite Mulled Punch (page 88).

THE ESSENTIAL SPIRITS AND MIXERS

Now, to the hard stuff. The drinks we chose to highlight in this compendium of recipes new and old were chosen not only for their seasonality—and a drink's ability to be craveable in cold weather—but also for their simplicity. We've limited the use of complicated syrups or infusions. We've also limited the number and types of ingredients to those any home bartender might reasonably stock. Below is just about every ingredient you need to execute all seventy of the recipes in this book, along with a few brands in each category that we love.

Amaro

Amaro is a general term used to describe a number of styles of Italian bitter herbal liqueurs typically consumed as *digestivi*—that is, after-dinner drinks meant to aid digestion. They can range from bittersweet to astringently bitter to cooling and herbal. For the purposes of mixing, you'll want to stock the rounder, sweeter Averna; the no-holds-barred bitter Fernet-Branca; the all-purpose utility player, Cynar; and cooling, alpine Braulio, which leans heavily on notes of mint. Think of these as either replacements for a sweetener or as your bitter salt and pepper. **Try:** Amaro Averna, Fernet-Branca, Cynar, and Amaro Braulio.

Apple Brandy

Apple brandy is simply a spirit made from fermented and distilled apples. A crucial ingredient in many early classic cocktails, it also happens to be a cool-weather go-to for many of today's modern bartenders. Apple brandy reaches its apex in the Calvados region of France, but for our drink-mixing purposes, look no further than New Jersey's own Laird's, which has been around since the late eighteenth century. **Try:** Laird's Apple Brandy 100.

Beer

For winter cocktails, be sure to have a not-too-hoppy pale ale and a stout on hand to dispatch in flips and cold-weather riffs on classics. **Try:** Sierra Nevada Pale Ale, Guinness, and Samuel Smith's Oatmeal Stout.

Cider

Both fresh-pressed apple cider and a dry, bubbly hard cider are winter bar essentials. The former can be used in punch-style and hot drinks, while the latter can be swapped into a spritz format or a highball for some cold-weather extra credit. **Try:** Bantam Wunderkind cider.

Cognac

A grape brandy distilled in the Cognac region of France, cognac was once a go-to spirit in the nascent years of American cocktailing, and is the base of important classics like the sidecar and the French 75. While V.S. and V.S.O.P. cognac can get very pricey, there are a number of excellent affordable options for mixing. **Try:** Pierre Ferrand 1840 Original Formula cognac and H by Hine V.S.O.P. cognac.

Gin

Gin is essentially a neutral grain spirit flavored with botanicals, specifically juniper. While London dry remains the most well-known (and most mixed with) style, the recent boom of craft gins has led to a broad range of flavor profiles under the umbrella of "gin." For our purposes, stocking a great London dry like Beefeater, and Plymouth Gin, a creamier, more citrus-forward historic gin brand, is about all you need on your winter bar. **Try:** Beefeater London Dry gin and Plymouth gin.

Other Liqueurs

Often referred to as "modifiers" in a drink, liqueurs are used in place of a sweetener or in small doses as "seasoners" in the recipes to follow. They range in profile from herbal and cooling to rich and brooding.

CHARTREUSE A historic French herbal liqueur made by Carthusian monks that's become a cult favorite among bartenders.

CHERRY HEERING A sweet and sour, dark-red Danish cherry liqueur that moonlights in drinks both classic and modern.

COINTREAU A historic brand of French triple sec (orange liqueur) also used as a sweetener or supporting player in cocktails.

CRÈME DE CACAO A chocolate liqueur used in more obscure classic cocktails and modern drinks seeking a bittersweet complexity, like the Sun Stealer (page 101) and the Barbary Coast (page 132).

CRÈME DE MENTHE Another once-crucial cocktail ingredient that is roaring back from obscurity to add a cooling lift to cocktails like Tom Macy's Peppermint Bark Eggnog (page 119).

ST. ELIZABETH ALLSPICE DRAM Built on the flavor of the allspice berry—which takes its name from its flavors of cinnamon, nutmeg, and clove—this historic liqueur is typically used in small doses to add a concentrated spice kick to a range of drinks.

ST-GERMAIN An elderflower liqueur from France typically used in place of a sweetener in cocktails.

Rum

Rum is a spirit made from fermented sugar cane juice or any of its byproducts, including molasses. There are almost no legal categories for production methods, save for rhum agricole, an appellation of the French West Indies, which must be made from fermented fresh cane juice. In the pages to follow, you'll find aged Jamaican rum called on frequently, as well as dark rum (made from molasses) and blackstrap rum (made from richer blackstrap molasses). **Try:** Appleton Estate Reserve Blend, Plantation Rum Original Dark, and Cruzan Black Strap Rum.

Sherry

Sherry is a fortified wine produced in a number of styles, from bone-dry to sticky sweet—all of them prime for mixing. The three dry styles most commonly called for in drinks are fino or manzanilla, amontillado, and oloroso. Fino and manzanilla (the latter is simply fino made in the town of Sanlúcar de Barrameda) derive their crisp, distinctive flavor from aging under a layer of yeast called *flor*, which protects the wine from oxygen. Amontillado is essentially an older fino or manzanilla that has aged both under flor and with the influence of oxygen, yielding a darker wine that's nuttier and more intensely savory. Oloroso, meanwhile, does not age under flor; instead, it's exposed to oxygen throughout the aging process, making for an even deeper nutty, savory profile and a texture that is much rounder than amontillado. For winter mixing, you'll also want to stock sweet Pedro Ximénez sherry, which can add depth and notes of figs, coffee, and chocolate in very small doses. Try swapping it into an old-fashioned in place of simple syrup. **Try:** Valdespino Inocente Fino, Hidalgo La Gitana Amontillado Napoleon, Gutierrez Colosia Sangre y Trabajadero Oloroso, and Valdespino Pedro Ximénez El Candado.

Tequila and Mezcal

Tequila is made in Mexico's Jalisco region from the heart (*piña*) of blue agave plants, which are steam-cooked, crushed, fermented, and distilled. Mezcal, meanwhile, is made from *piñas* of a number of agave species (wild and cultivated), primarily in the region of Oaxaca, that are roasted instead of steam-cooked, crushed, and distilled. The process of roasting the piña leads to a distinct smoky flavor profile. While there are aged versions of both tequila and mezcal, we stick to unaged versions of both for mixing. **Try:** Del Maguey Vida mezcal, Sombra Mezcal, Tapatio Tequila Blanco, and Tequila Ocho Plata.

Vermouth

Fortified wines infused with various botanicals, vermouths play a vital role in just about every style of cocktail. The three main styles of vermouth are sweet (rosso or rouge), dry, and blanc (bianco), and all are essential. Sweet vermouth, which originated in Turin, Italy, is darker in color and typically expresses sweet spice and vanilla notes. Dry and blanc vermouth originated in Marseilles and Chambéry, France, respectively; both styles are nearly clear in color and tend to be more herbal in character. Look for Dolin from Chambéry and Carpano and Martini & Rossi from Turin; these houses produce excellent vermouths in all three styles. **Try:** Carpano, Martini & Rossi, and Dolin.

Whiskey

There are few spirits better suited to winter drinking than whiskey (or "whisky" if it comes from Scotland, Japan, or Canada). Here are the three styles represented in the recipes to follow.

BOURBON The most widely recognized American variety of whiskey, bourbon is distilled from a fermented mash that contains at least 51 percent corn. The result tends to be sweeter and rounder in texture than both rye and scotch. For our money, it is always the best choice when building a hot whiskey drink, or as a companion to drinks that already have a strong spice component. Try: Old Grand-Dad Bonded Kentucky Straight Bourbon Whiskey, Evan Williams Single Barrel, and Buffalo Trace Kentucky Straight Bourbon.

RYE This American whiskey must be distilled from a fermented mash that contains at least 51 percent rye grain. Rye tends to be a little spicier and leaner than bourbon, and it is our preferred culprit in classics like the Manhattan and the whiskey sour. **Try:** Wild Turkey Rye, Old Overholt Straight Rye Whiskey (for a lower-proof option), and Rittenhouse Rye 100.

SCOTCH Scotch is a single-malt (made from 100 percent malted barley) whisky produced in six designated regions in Scotland—each with its own distinct identity and corresponding flavor profile, though there is much diversity within each region. Some are smoky (Islay) and some are high-toned and fruity (Highlands). For the purposes of mixing in winter, it's always good to have a high-quality blended scotch on hand that shows just a bit of smoky (or "peaty" as it's called) complexity alongside a more aggressively peated Islay Scotch from the likes of Ardbeg or Laphroaig. **Try:** Dewar's 12 Year The Ancestor Blended Scotch Whisky, Monkey Shoulder Blended Scotch Whisky , and Laphroaig Islay Single Malt Scotch Whisky.

Wine

Whether it be red wine as the base of a punch-style drink or champagne to top your winter spritz, champagne cocktail, or French 75, one should never be without a stainless steel–aged (tannins are not your friend when it comes to mixing), juicy red wine, and a selection of bubbles.

In place of champagne, stock a more affordable dry Crémant d'Alsace for drinks that call for top-shelf bubbly. For all other bubbly cocktails, a prosecco will do. A couple of these recipes also call for Lambrusco as a cool-weather-appropriate tag-in for your standard bubbly. **Try:** Albert Mann Crémant d'Alsace Brut, Sorelle Bronca Extra Dry Prosecco, and Lini 910 Lambrusco Rosso.

TOOLS

While you could fill an entire kitchen with all manner of specialty drinkware and tools, below you'll find the basics you'll need to stock a proper winter bar.

BARSPOON This long spoon, typically with a spiraled midsection used for coiling citrus peels, is a requisite for stirred drinks. It's also used in recipes as a unit of measurement.

CHEESECLOTH Typically used to remove curds from whey in cheesemaking, cheesecloth works well to strain out solids in everything from horchata to milk punch.

COCKTAIL SHAKER The Boston shaker is a two-piece set of tins—one smaller tin nestled into the larger. We prefer it over a three-piece cobbler shaker, which has a built-in strainer. It's both easier to clean and generally larger in volume, allowing you to shake multiple drinks at once.

FINE-MESH STRAINER This is typically employed in conjunction with a Hawthorne strainer (see page 34) when a recipe, generally one with muddled fruit or herbs, calls for "fine straining" to ensure that no solids make their way into the finished drink.

CONTINUED ON PAGE 34

INFUSED SPIRITS

Have only a few basics on hand and need to add some flavor with a capital F? That's the perfect setting for a spirit infusion, one where it can be the star. For us, it's always helpful to look to the spirit infusion that launched a thousand infusions: the Benton's bacon-infused bourbon that was dispatched in the now modern-classic Benton's old-fashioned at the famous New York bar PDT. The rich, smoky flavor and buttery texture of the spirit was a revelation, and stands as a lesson in infusing to make less work for yourself, not more. Here are a few winter-appropriate spirit infusions to use in any number of classic cocktail templates (see page 3) to max effect.

A FEW TIPS

Begin with a small quantity of spirit and work up. Spirits at 80 proof or more take to infusions quickly— before you double-down with a full-bottle infusion, start with a cup and then scale up if you like it.

Don't forget to strain. Make sure to properly strain out all solids using cheesecloth (we fold it over to double up for extra insurance) or a coffee filter. If you still see solids after the first strain, do it again— removing all solids will avoid any off-flavors or instability.

Borrow from your favorite foods. Start with flavor combinations that are tried-and-true in the kitchen and extend those to booze. It's really about what sounds good to you, combined with a bit of technique

EARL GREY GIN

ADAPTED FROM AUDREY SAUNDERS, PEGU CLUB, NEW YORK

4 tablespoons loose Earl Grey tea   1 (750 ml) bottle gin,
                                           preferably Tanqueray

Add the tea to the bottle, cap, and shake. Let sit at room temperature for 2 hours. Strain through a fine-mesh sieve or coffee filter into a bowl. Transfer to a clean bottle and store indefinitely at room temperature.

CINNAMON APPLE BRANDY

8 cinnamon sticks, crushed   1 (750 ml) bottle Laird's Apple Brandy 100

Add the cinnamon sticks to the bottle, cap, and shake. Let sit at room temperature for 4 days. Strain through a fine-mesh sieve or coffee filter into a bowl. Rinse out the bottle to remove any debris, then pour the infusion back into the clean bottle. Store indefinitely at room temperature.

BROWNED BUTTER BOURBON

½ cup (1 stick) unsalted butter   1 (750 ml) bottle bourbon

Heat the butter in a skillet over medium heat until it begins to foam and caramelize, about 5 minutes (don't let it burn; it can happen quickly). Remove the pan from the heat and let the butter cool.

Funnel the bourbon and butter into a wide-mouthed jar, shake vigorously, and let stand at room temperature for 3 hours. Move it to the freezer for 2 to 3 hours, until the butter has hardened on top of the spirit. Remove the layer of butter, strain the mixture through a cheesecloth or coffee filter into a clean bottle, and store in the refrigerator for up to 6 months.

HAWTHORNE STRAINER Flat, and affixed with a spiral coil, this strainer is typically fitted to a tin to strain shaken drinks, but it can also do double-duty with most mixing glasses.

LEWIS BAG This heavy-duty canvas bag with a drawstring at one end is used to crushed ice at home. Simply stuff it with regular cubes and whack it with anything you please.

MICROPLANE Plenty of grated nutmeg and cinnamon are in your future. It's worth investing in a high-quality Microplane for all your eggnog needs.

MIXING GLASS When mixing stirred drinks you can rely on a regular old pint glass, but we suggest investing in a crystal mixing glass—we love the Yarai line from Cocktail Kingdom—if you want to up your game.

MUDDLER The baton-shaped muddler is typically used for mashing fresh citrus and herbs into sugar before shaking. While most kitchen stores peddle metal or plastic muddlers, we recommend sticking with the classic wooden version.

Y-SHAPED PEELER While a vertical peeler will suffice, the y-shaped peeler is your best bet if you intend to peel your way to many a perfect citrus garnish.

GLASSWARE

The basics—rocks glass, collins glass, coupe, tempered mug—will get you most of the way in winter, but here is the full list of drinkware called for in the recipes to follow.

COLLINS AND HIGHBALL GLASSES These "chimney-style" glasses are used for "long" drinks—that is, those lengthened with a nonalcoholic mixer, typically bubbly water. The collins is thinner and taller than the highball glass.

COUPE Having largely replaced the V-shaped cocktail glass in bars around the country, the rounded coupe is the most common glass called for in drinks served "up" (that is, without ice), both shaken and stirred.

FLUTE The tall, narrow glass of choice for classic champagne cocktails like the French 75, champagne cocktail, and other festive bubbly drinks.

IRISH COFFEE GLASS Irish coffee is so important to the canon of winter drinks that it even has its own glass. It's shaped like a curvaceous sour glass and set atop a short, ornate stem. Irish coffee is also sometimes served in a handled mug of similar design.

MULE MUG This copper mug has almost become more well-known than the drink that made it famous. Almost. While typically associated with the Moscow mule, these head-turning mugs can house any drink you please, mule or otherwise.

NICK AND NORA Shaped like a coupe but with a longer stem and smaller bowl, the Nick and Nora (named for the husband and wife detective duo in the 1934 film *The Thin Man* and its sequels) has rushed back onto the scene to become an increasingly common sight.

PUNCH BOWL The flowing bowl is the very definition of holiday drinking. While you can repurpose a large serving bowl for punch, we recommend investing in a proper punch bowl and cups—extra points if it's vintage.

ROCKS AND DOUBLE ROCKS GLASS The rocks glass (aka, the old-fashioned glass) is synonymous with strong and stirred cocktails, like the Negroni and the old-fashioned, but it's hardly limited to them. The double rocks glass is larger by volume with a capacity of 10 to 12 ounces versus the 6 to 8 ounces of a standard rocks glass.

SOUR GLASS Often resembling a squat flute glass or more angular coupe, the sour glass is often called for in egg-white sours and whole-egg drinks, like flips.

TEMPERED MUG OR TODDY MUG These durable, clear mugs made of tempered glass are designed to withstand high heat.

WINTER
COCKTAIL
RECIPES

OLD-FASHIONED

A simple mix of spirits, sugar, bitters, and water, the old-fashioned made its appearance in 1806 as the first printed recipe for a cocktail ("cock tail"), but it wasn't named until later that century when more ostentatious new-fangled cocktails entered the canon. In fact, during Prohibition, the old-fashioned nearly lost its humble footing when the recipe veered into odd territory, with the addition of fruit and cherries to distract from the crude spirits available at the time. After repeal, the imposter version stuck until the recent cocktail revival brought the original recipe back from the brink of extinction.

1 sugar cube, or 1 barspoon simple syrup (page 23)

2 dashes Angostura bitters

A splash of warm water (if using a sugar cube)

2 ounces rye or bourbon whiskey

Garnish orange twist

If using a sugar cube, muddle the cube with the Angostura bitters and a small splash of warm water in a double rocks glass until dissolved. If using simple syrup, swirl with the bitters in a double rocks glass. Add the whiskey and ice (preferably an oversized cube) and stir well. Garnish with an orange twist.

HOT TODDY

Though the modern definition of the toddy almost always points to any alcoholic beverage served hot, it wasn't always so. One of the ancestral drinks of the cocktail world, the toddy's traditional formula loosely meant a base spirit (usually rum or whiskey), plus a sweetener, served either hot or cold. There were some medicinal connotations for the practice, especially when it included citrus. Today the usage encompasses a wide swath of drinks that swings from the most basic recipe of a base spirit plus sugar to more complex iterations. This version is a template prime for riffing with a base of any dark spirit, plus hot water, citrus, sweetener, and spices.

1½ ounces bourbon or rye whiskey (or any dark spirit, including aged rum or cognac)

¾ ounce honey or pure maple syrup

½ ounce freshly squeezed lemon juice

4 to 5 ounces hot water

Garnish lemon wheel and cinnamon stick

Combine the spirit, honey, and lemon juice in a tempered mug. Top with hot water and stir gently to dissolve the honey. Garnish with a lemon wheel and a cinnamon stick.

MANHATTAN
(ROB ROY)

Two cocktails every American knows by name are undoubtedly the martini and its dark and deep ally, the Manhattan. The heady duo both rely on a solid spirituous base amplified by vermouth (dry for the martini, sweet for the Manhattan), and are recognized by their signature garnishes: typically olives for the former, and a brandied cherry for the latter. Over the course of the twentieth century, the martini largely pulled back on the vermouth, becoming ever drier, but the Manhattan has remained resolute in its ratio. If you're more of a scotch drinker, swap it into the formula in place of the rye and you've got another classic, the Rob Roy.

2 ounces rye or
bourbon whiskey

1 ounce sweet vermouth

2 dashes Angostura bitters

Garnish brandied cherry
or a lemon twist

Combine the whiskey, vermouth, and bitters in a mixing glass. Add ice and stir well. Strain into a chilled coupe. Garnish with a brandied cherry.

NEGRONI
(BOULEVARDIER, OLD PAL)

Like many good stories, the one about the Negroni involves rakish Italian nobility. Most accounts credit the recipe to one Count Negroni, a swashbuckling proto-boho who reportedly spent time as a rodeo cowboy in the United States. Compounding his wild ways, legend has it that back at a bar in Italy in 1919, he asked for something like an Americano but boozier. Swap gin for soda water, and presto: the Negroni. Navigating a tightrope between bitter and sweet, this powerful drink—a study in balance—has evolved into one of the cornerstones of the classic cocktail revival. You can substitute rye whiskey for gin and sweet vermouth for dry to make an Old Pal, or substitute 1½ ounces of rye or bourbon in place of gin for a Boulevardier.

1 ounce gin   1 ounce sweet vermouth
1 ounce Campari   Garnish orange twist

Combine the gin, Campari, and vermouth in a mixing glass. Add ice and stir until chilled. To serve on the rocks, strain over ice into a rocks glass. To serve up, strain into a chilled coupe or cocktail glass. Garnish with an orange twist.

FRENCH 75

History says that this champagne cocktail originated at Harry's New York Bar in Paris in the early 1900s, but it was co-opted and made legendary shortly thereafter by Arnaud's French 75 bar in New Orleans. The original recipe calls for cognac combined with champagne, lemon juice, and sugar, but somewhere along the line, it became fashionable to make the drink with gin instead. Arnaud's stays the course with cognac, which gives the cocktail more depth and a little bit of spice, making it a great bubbly drink for the fall and winter. The livelier gin version (a gin sour royale, really) is best in warm weather.

2 ounces cognac or gin

½ ounce freshly squeezed lemon juice

¼ ounce simple syrup (page 23)

3 ounces champagne or other dry sparkling wine

Garnish long, curly lemon twist

Combine the cognac, lemon juice, and simple syrup in a cocktail shaker. Add ice and shake until chilled. Strain into a coupe or a flute and top with sparkling wine. Garnish with a long, curly twist of lemon.

SAZERAC

Born in the mid-1800s at the Sazerac Coffee House in New Orleans, this cocktail has been a beloved stalwart ever since. While some claim the drink was originally made with cognac, that theory has largely been dismissed. The Sazerac's alluring aromatic intensity—anise, peppery rye, and spiced Peychaud's bitters—make this one of the most beloved drinks in the canon of classic cocktails, and a drink perfectly suited to winter drinking.

1 barspoon absinthe

2 ounces rye whiskey

½ ounce simple syrup (page 23)

2 dashes Peychaud's bitters

Garnish lemon twist

Combine a barspoon of absinthe and ice in a rocks glass and swirl to coat. Discard. In a mixing glass, combine the whiskey, simple syrup, and bitters. Add ice, stir, and strain the mixture into the prepared rocks glass. Garnish with a lemon twist.

MARTINI

Considering all of the sleuthing done by cocktail historians, it's remarkable that no one has turned up a solid story for the birth of the martini. Certain facts, however, have been established: the martini postdated the Manhattan and probably evolved from a mix of sweet vermouth and sweet gin as drier versions of those alcohols became popular at the turn of the twentieth century. Over time, bitters and vermouth both fell out of fashion, and the ratio of the drink tilted strongly to gin. The cocktail revival has righted some of these wrong turns, but there now exists a world of permutations regarding the ratio of vermouth to gin, garnishing with an olive or a twist, and even, yes, shaken or stirred. For the most authentic version: your choice, your choice, stirred.

2 ounces gin

1 ounce dry vermouth, preferably Dolin

2 dashes orange bitters

Garnish lemon twist or olive

Combine the gin, vermouth, and bitters in a mixing glass. Add ice and stir until chilled. Strain into a chilled coupe. Garnish with a lemon twist or olive.

WHISKEY SOUR
(BOSTON SOUR, NEW YORK SOUR)

The template for this iconic sour—whiskey, lemon juice, and sugar, shaken with ice—has laid the foundation for many cocktails due to its structural, unadorned simplicity. Merely adding an egg white (creating what's known as a Boston sour) gives the drink a bit more texture and lift. Remove the egg white and add a red wine float to transform it into the New York sour, a variation that popped up in the late 1800s.

2 ounces bourbon or rye whiskey

¾ ounce freshly squeezed lemon juice

¾ ounce simple syrup (page 23)

Garnish orange half wheels and a brandied cherry

Combine all the ingredients in a cocktail shaker and dry shake (shake without ice). Add ice to the shaker and shake well. Strain into a chilled coupe or into a rocks glass over ice and garnish with orange half-wheels and a brandied cherry.

HOT BUTTERED RUM

Hot. Buttered. Rum. Is there anything sexier than a glass of warm, golden spirit mixed with melted butter? No, we think not. Americans have been whipping up a spiced butter batter and dousing it with rum and hot water since before they were Americans. This version brings the winter warmer to its full velvety potential. **SERVES 4**

½ cup (1 stick) butter, room temperature
¾ cup packed brown sugar
1 teaspoon ground cinnamon
¼ teaspoon freshly grated nutmeg
⅛ teaspoon ground allspice

⅛ teaspoon salt
pinch of cayenne pepper
2 cups hot water
1 cup dark rum
Garnish 4 star anise pods, 4 cinnamon sticks, and 4 clove-studded lemon twists

Combine the butter, brown sugar, cinnamon, nutmeg, allspice, cloves, salt, and cayenne in a mixing bowl and blend with an electric mixer. Refrigerate the batter until ready to use.

When ready to serve, prep mugs by filling with hot water to warm them. Let stand for a minute or two, and discard. Add 2 tablespoons of batter to each prepped mug. Pour in 2 ounces hot water and stir to mix. Add 2 ounces of rum to each mug, and then top with 2 more ounces of hot water. Stir to combine and garnish with a star anise pod, cinnamon stick, and clove-studded lemon twist.

CHAMPAGNE COCKTAIL

Swap champagne for whiskey in the old-fashioned template, and you'll get this pedigreed cocktail, which was first mentioned in Jerry Thomas's 1862 *How to Mix Drinks*. Its low-alcohol and bubbly constitution make this recipe a good candidate for winter day drinking. The question as to whether you pony up for the real stuff or choose a another dry sparkling wine depends largely on your opinion of the sanctity of champagne.

1 sugar cube, or
1 barspoon sugar

3 dashes Angostura bitters

Champagne or other dry
sparkling wine, to top

Garnish long, curly lemon twist
(optional)

Add the sugar cube or sugar to a flute. Dash Angostura bitters over the sugar to soak. Slowly top up with champagne. Garnish with a long, curly twist of lemon.

CRANBERRY SMASH

Editors of PUNCH, New York

A variation on the beloved whiskey smash (itself a variation on the mint julep), our smash goes full fall/winter with the addition of muddled cranberry and citrus and the bonus kick of spicy Angostura bitters, shaken and served over a festive mound of crushed ice.

1 ounce simple syrup (page 23)

2 lemon wedges

5 or 6 cranberries, fresh or frozen

2 ounces bourbon or gin

2 dashes Angostura bitters

Garnish skewered cranberries

Combine the simple syrup, lemon wedges, and cranberries in a cocktail shaker and use a muddler to lightly crush the cranberries. Add the bourbon and bitters, then add ice and shake well. Pour through a fine-mesh strainer over crushed ice into a rocks glass and garnish with skewered cranberries.

FILIBUSTER

Erik Adkins, Slanted Door Group, San Francisco

The Filibuster is proof of just how simple it is to slightly alter the classic whiskey sour formula to give it extra season-appropriate depth. Swap out simple syrup for rich maple syrup, and you get this rich, burnished riff on the classic.

2 ounces rye whiskey

¾ ounce freshly squeezed lemon juice

½ ounce pure maple syrup

1 small egg white

Garnish Angostura bitters

Combine the whiskey, lemon juice, maple syrup, and egg white in a cocktail shaker and dry shake (shake without ice). Add ice and shake well. Strain into a chilled coupe. To garnish, dash Angostura bitters decoratively over the top.

BLINKER

Adapted by the Editors of PUNCH, New York

The first known mention of the oddball three-ingredient cocktail comes from Patrick Gavin Duffy's *The Official Mixer's Manual* (1934) in these proportions. We discovered it thanks to Robert Simonson's *3-Ingredient Cocktails*, and have since worked it into our winter playlist. What seems like an ill-fated drink on paper is actually an oddly satisfying (and simple) bitter-tart-spicy mashup.

3 ounces freshly squeezed grapefruit juice

2 ounces rye whiskey

1 ounce grenadine, preferably Jack Rudy

Garnish grapefruit twist

Combine the grapefruit juice, whiskey, and grenadine in a cocktail shaker filled with ice and shake until chilled. Strain into a chilled coupe. Express a grapefruit twist over the drink and drop into the glass.

ALABAZAM

Adapted by Jamie Boudreau, Canon, Seattle

American expatriate Leo Engel was working at the Criterion Hotel in London when he supposedly created the Alabazam, an obscure recipe that appears in his 1878 book, *American and Other Drinks*. The drink is basically a brandy sour, aromatized with a heavy dose of bitters alongside the citrus tang of Cointreau.

1½ ounces cognac

½ ounce Cointreau

¼ ounce Angostura bitters

¼ ounce freshly squeezed lemon juice

¼ ounce simple syrup (page 23)

Combine all the ingredients in a cocktail shaker. Add ice and shake until chilled. Strain into chilled coupe. Marvel at the spiciness.

MOTT AND MULBERRY

Leo Robitschek, The NoMad Bar, New York

Named for an intersection on the border of Little Italy and Chinatown in New York City, the Mott and Mulberry is an autumnal whiskey sour riff. The mix of spicy rye, bittersweet amaro, and tart apple cider layered over demerara syrup and fresh lemon combine for a bone-warming comfort cocktail.

1 ounce rye whiskey

1 ounce Luxardo Amaro Abano

¾ ounce fresh-pressed apple cider or tart apple juice

½ ounce freshly squeezed lemon juice

½ ounce demerara syrup (see Note)

Garnish thin apple slices

Combine the whiskey, amaro, apple cider, lemon juice, and demerara syrup in a cocktail shaker. Add ice and shake until chilled. Strain into a rocks glass over ice. Garnish with thin apple slices.

NOTE To make demerara syrup, follow the recipe for simple syrup (page 23), substituting rich demerara sugar for regular cane sugar.

GLASGOW MULE

Damon Boelte, Grand Army Bar, New York

The classic mule, or buck, is composed of a base spirit, citrus, and ginger ale or ginger beer. The Glasgow Mule is built on a scotch foundation (hence the name) that is kicked up with floral St-Germain and two types of spice, by way of Angostura bitters and Fever-Tree ginger beer. The effect is a mule—a staple of warm-weather drinking—dressed up for winter.

4 ounces ginger beer, preferably Fever-Tree

1½ ounces blended scotch

¾ ounce freshly squeezed lemon juice

½ ounce St-Germain

1 dash Angostura bitters

Garnish lemon wheel (optional) and candied ginger

Combine the ginger beer, scotch, lemon juice, St-Germain and bitters in a large mule mug or a tall collins glass. Add crushed ice and stir gently to mix. Garnish with a lemon wheel and candied ginger.

MIDNIGHT STINGER

Sam Ross, Attaboy, New York

For those of us who like to counter winter with a combination of whiskey, citrus, and a bitter component (and at PUNCH, we do), our go-to is this bitter take on the whiskey sour, which calls for a full ounce of bracing Fernet-Branca. Be advised that this is not for the faint of heart—and that's exactly why we love it.

1 ounce bourbon

1 ounce Fernet-Branca

¾ ounce freshly squeezed lemon juice

¾ ounce simple syrup (page 23)

Garnish mint sprig

Combine the bourbon, Fernet-Branca, lemon juice, and simple syrup in a cocktail shaker. Add ice and shake. Strain over crushed ice into a rocks glass and garnish with a mint sprig.

ROSEMARY GIN AND TONIC

Editors of PUNCH, New York

The classic gin and tonic gets winterized with the addition of aromatic rosemary and quick-and-easy grapefruit shrub, making it a more appropriate cool-weather companion than the original.

1 sprig rosemary	½ ounce freshly squeezed lime juice
¾ ounce grapefruit shrub (page 19)	4 ounces tonic
2 ounces gin	**Garnish** sprig of rosemary and grapefruit wheels

Remove the stem from the rosemary and combine with the shrub in a cocktail shaker. Use a muddler to lightly crush the rosemary. Add the gin, lime juice, and ice, and shake to chill. Pour through a fine-mesh strainer into an ice-filled tall collins glass and top with tonic. Garnish with a sprig of rosemary and grapefruit wheels.

WINTER MOJITO

Editors of PUNCH, New York

Our position on the mojito is that it need not be relegated to the warmer months. If you consider its simple combination of fresh herbs, sugar, citrus, rum, and soda water, it's easy to slot in alternative herbs and a richer spirit for a winter revamp. In our cold-weather version we sub out white rum for rich, brooding blackstrap and mint for muddled rosemary.

1 large sprig rosemary

¾ ounce simple syrup (page 23) or winter herb syrup (page 24; see Note)

2 ounces blackstrap rum

1 ounce freshly squeezed lime juice

Soda water, to top

Garnish lime wheel and rosemary sprig

Remove the stem from the sprig of the rosemary and combine with the simple syrup in a cocktail shaker. Use a muddler to lightly crush the rosemary and let sit for a few minutes. Add the rum and lime juice. Add ice, shake, and pour through a fine-mesh strainer into a collins glass over ice. Top with soda and garnish with a lime wheel and a sprig of rosemary.

NOTE If you use winter herb syrup, you need not muddle the rosemary.

IMPROVED STONE FENCE

Editors of PUNCH, New York

Before raiding Fort Ticonderoga in 1775 at the beginning of the
Revolutionary War, Ethan Allen and the Green Mountain Boys
went drinking at the Remington Tavern in Castleton, where they
knocked back a mixture of rum and hard cider called a Stone
Fence. When Allen stormed the officers' quarters and demanded
they surrender, the English didn't offer Allen much resistance
and Fort Ticonderoga was successfully seized, thanks in part—
we like to think—to the fortifying Stone Fence. Our version
of the classic cider-and-rum (or whiskey or brandy) cocktail
adds both lemon juice and Angostura bitters to a base of funky
Jamaican rum.

3 ounces fresh-pressed
apple cider

2 ounces Jamaican rum

¾ ounce freshly
squeezed lemon juice

3 dashes Angostura bitters

Garnish freshly grated
nutmeg, apple fan

Combine the cider, rum, lemon juice, and bitters in a cocktail
shaker. Add ice and shake briefly. Strain over ice into a double
rocks glass and garnish with nutmeg and an apple fan.

KING'S CROSS

Dan Sabo, Paligroup Management, Los Angeles

While unorthodox on paper, this ode to Scottish Islay-born gin and peated scotch is a crowd-pleasing mix of savory (smoky scotch), floral (chamomile and honey), and herbal (sage, gin) elements. It's light and nuanced enough to pair with a motley holiday spread and spirituous enough that it's firmly rooted in the winter drink matrix. **SERVES 8**

12 ounces gin, preferably The Botanist gin

8 ounces freshly squeezed lemon juice

6 ounces honey syrup (page 23)

6 ounces chamomile tea, chilled

2 ounces peated Islay scotch

24 ounces soda water

Garnish 20 sage leaves, 12 lemon wheels

Combine the gin, lemon juice, honey syrup, tea, and scotch in a punch bowl. Add a few small cubes and stir until chilled. Once cold, add a large block of ice, then add the soda water. Garnish the bowl with sage leaves and lemon wheels, and ladle punch into cups to serve.

RED QUEEN

Editors of PUNCH, New York

Inspired by a number of early twentieth-century recipes for long drinks that rely on a base of red wine, the Red Queen gets extra fortification from the addition of both bourbon and Amaro Braulio, an alpine amaro that adds a cooling, herbal freshness to the drink. As for the name, it's a reference to a line in the Jefferson Airplane song "White Rabbit."

3 ounces red wine	½ ounce simple syrup (page 23)
1 ounce bourbon	½ ounce Amaro Braulio
¾ ounce freshly squeezed lemon juice	**Garnish** lemon wheels, fresh thyme, sage, and rosemary

Combine the wine, bourbon, lemon juice, simple syrup, and amaro in a cocktail shaker. Add ice, shake, and strain over crushed ice into a tall collins glass. Garnish with lemon wheels, fresh thyme, sage, and rosemary.

HIGH ALTITUDE HIGHBALL

Ryan Fitzgerald, ABV, San Francisco

At PUNCH we're big fans of the Japanese whisky highball—a combination of chilled sparkling water and Japanese whisky served tall over ice. Here the staple gets an extra dose of complexity from the alpine herbal liqueur génépy, paired with Hakushu whisky, which also hails from a mountain region. Double the alpine flavor, double the fun.

1½ ounces Japanese whisky, preferably Hakushu

½ ounce génépy, preferably Dolin Génépy des Alpes

6 ounces soda water

Garnish long lemon twist

Combine the whisky and génépy in a tall collins glass. Top with soda and garnish with a long twist of lemon.

WINTER PALOMA

Editors of PUNCH, New York

The Mexican classic the paloma—essentially the love child of
a greyhound and a margarita—gets dressed up in a winter coat,
courtesy of the addition of sage. The hardy winter herb cameos
in the traditional formula by way of fresh sage leaves, turning the
summer classic into the kind of cocktail that feels right at home
beside the fire.

3 large sage leaves

¾ ounce simple syrup
(page 23)

2 ounces mezcal

¾ ounce freshly squeezed
ruby red grapefruit juice

¾ ounce freshly
squeezed lime juice

Soda water, to top

Garnish sage sprig

Combine the sage leaves and simple syrup in a cocktail shaker
and use a muddler to lightly crush the sage. Add the mezcal,
grapefruit juice, and lime juice. Shake with ice, strain into
a tall collins glass over ice, top with soda water, and garnish
with a sprig of sage.

THE MYSTICAL ONE

Natasha David, Nitecap, New York

This simple, holiday-ready rendition of a whiskey sour combines the one-two punch of sage and cinnamon alongside lime juice in place of lemon. If you're angling for a bit more richness, add a small egg white to the mix and shake extra vigorously to combine.

3 sage leaves

½ ounce cinnamon syrup (page 21)

¾ ounce freshly squeezed lime juice

2 ounces bourbon

Garnish sage leaf

Combine the 3 sage leaves and the cinnamon syrup in a cocktail shaker and use a muddler to lightly crush the sage. Add the lime juice and bourbon. Add ice and shake until chilled. Strain into a coupe and garnish with a sage leaf.

DAVY JONES'S LOCKER

Brad Farran, Durham

Davy Jones's Locker is a nineteenth-century sailors' euphemism for the bottom of the ocean, or death by drowning. This drink began with the classic daiquiri and was winterized using rich Jamaican rum, Fernet-Branca, and a nod to the iconic grapefruit-cinnamon tiki syrup Donn's Mix.

2 ounces gold rum, preferably Appleton Estate Reserve Blend

1 ounce freshly squeezed grapefruit juice

½ ounce cinnamon syrup (page 21)

¼ ounce Fernet-Branca

¼ ounce freshly squeezed lime juice

Garnish lime wheel

Combine the rum, grapefruit juice, cinnamon syrup, Fernet-Branca, and lime juice in a cocktail shaker. Add ice, shake until chilled, and strain into a small wineglass or coupe. Garnish with a lime wheel.

SAIGON LADY

Lucinda Sterling, Middle Branch, New York

This rich sour was built around the flavor of Saigon cinnamon, which is more potently aromatic (think Red Hots) than your standard Ceylon cinnamon. The base of the drink is split between blended scotch (look for something lightly peated, like Black Grouse or Monkey Shoulder) and brandy, then balanced with lemon juice, tart grenadine, egg white, and a finishing dust of cinnamon. It has all the hallmarks of a holiday-appropriate sour.

1 ounce blended scotch

1 ounce brandy

¾ ounce grenadine, preferably Jack Rudy

¾ ounce freshly squeezed lemon juice

1 egg white

Garnish grated cinnamon

Combine the scotch, brandy, grenadine, lemon juice, and egg white in a cocktail shaker and dry shake (shake without ice). Add ice, shake until chilled, and strain over ice into a rocks glass. Garnish with grated cinnamon.

SANGUINELLO SPRITZ

Editors of PUNCH, New York

The spritz—the bitter, bubbly, low-alcohol icon of Italian aperitivo culture—is a perfect candidate for riffing and experimentation. This wintry adaptation wrangles the holiday season with the addition of in-season blood orange, spicy Barolo Chinato (a lightly bitter aromatized wine), and vanilla syrup for a spritz with enough stuffing to stand up to the season.

1 ounce Cocchi Barolo Chinato

1 ounce freshly squeezed blood orange juice

½ ounce Campari

½ ounce vanilla syrup (page 23)

Prosecco, to top

Garnish blood orange half-wheel

Combine the Barolo Chinato, orange juice, Campari, and vanilla syrup in a cocktail shaker. Add ice and shake until chilled. Strain over ice into a tall collins glass and top with prosecco. Garnish with a blood orange half-wheel.

BOOZE + JUICE

Diamond Reef, Brooklyn

The Booze + Juice is a triumph of seasonal minimalism. In the original version served at Brooklyn's Diamond Reef, the drink pairs fresh-pressed Granny Smith apple juice with your spirit of choice; we at PUNCH tend to favor whiskey (with mezcal a close second).

2 ounces rye or bourbon whiskey	1 Granny Smith apple, juiced

Combine whiskey and fresh apple juice in a tall collins glass. Add ice and enjoy.

JEREZ FLYER

Editors of PUNCH, New York

The Jerez Flyer is a mashup of one of our favorite winter punches and a hat tip to history, honoring the trade between Spain's sherry region and the American colonies. It leans on American apple brandy (a colonial staple) and dry amontillado sherry, kicked up with lemon juice and a pinch of cayenne pepper, the latter of which adds an extra warming dimension to the drink.

1 ounce amontillado sherry

1 ounce apple brandy, preferably Laird's Apple Brandy 100

¾ ounce freshly squeezed lemon juice

¾ ounce simple syrup (page 23)

Pinch of cayenne pepper

Garnish thin quarter-slice of apple

Combine the sherry, brandy, lemon juice, simple syrup, and cayenne in a cocktail shaker. Add ice, shake, and strain into a coupe. Garnish with a thin quarter-slice of apple.

WINTER PIMM'S CUP

Editors of PUNCH, New York

While there is no official category for ostentatiously garnished classics, we refer to them as "chain-reaction drinks." One hits the bar and, soon, everyone's drinking one. The Pimm's Cup— a simple mix of Pimm's No. 1 liqueur and ginger ale, garnished with abandon—is one of those drinks. Here we replace ginger ale with American lager and then garnish the drink with a bounty of fresh winter herbs, apples, and cranberries for a head-turning holiday take on the classic summertime cooler.

1-inch piece ginger, peeled and chopped

¾ ounce simple syrup (page 23)

2 ounces Pimm's No. 1

¾ ounce freshly squeezed lemon juice

American lager, to top

Garnish seasonal fruit and herbs

Combine the ginger and simple syrup in a cocktail shaker and use a muddler to lightly crush the ginger. Add the Pimm's and lemon juice. Add ice, shake, strain over ice into a tall collins glass, and top with lager. Garnish with seasonal fruit and herbs.

MULLED PUNCH

Jason Kosmas, The 86 Co., New York

This garnet-hued punch mixes a DIY holiday tea syrup with fizzy, fruity Lambrusco and vodka (though it also works with whiskey). It's a dangerously easy-drinking crowd-pleaser. **SERVES 12 TO 16**

1 (750 ml) bottle vodka, preferably Aylesbury Duck

12 ounces freshly squeezed lemon juice

12 ounces Holiday Spice Tea Syrup (recipe follows)

6 ounces water

1 750 ml bottle dry Lambrusco

Garnish 12 to 16 orange wheels studded with cloves (optional)

In a large punch bowl, combine the vodka, lemon juice, tea syrup, and water. Add a large block of ice (or large ice cubes), then stir to combine. Add the Lambrusco just before serving and give the punch a gentle stir to mix. Garnish with orange wheels studded with whole cloves.

HOLIDAY SPICE TEA SYRUP

2 bags holiday spice tea

3 cups sugar

Steep tea bags in 1½ cups boiling water for 3 to 5 minutes. Remove bags, add sugar, and stir to fully dissolve. Allow to cool. Store in a glass jar in the fridge for up to 1 month. **MAKES 2 CUPS**

REVOLVER

Jon Santer, Bourbon & Branch, San Francisco

Introduced at the venerable San Francisco speakeasy Bourbon & Branch, the Revolver has since become a modern classic. Built on a base of spicy rye-heavy Bulleit bourbon and local St. George Spirits NOLA Coffee Liqueur, this riff on the old-fashioned is then finished off with a flamed orange twist, which adds a layer of smoky aromatic complexity.

2 ounces bourbon, preferably Bulleit

½ ounce coffee liqueur, preferably St. George Spirits

2 dashes orange bitters

Garnish flamed orange twist (see Note)

Combine the bourbon, coffee liqueur, and bitters in a mixing glass. Add ice and stir until chilled. Strain into a chilled coupe. Flame an orange twist, then drop the twist into the drink.

NOTE To flame an orange twist, take a thick piece of orange peel and angle its skin side just above the drink. Light a match and hold it in front of the peel, and squeeze to express its oils over the flame and the drink.

LATIN TRIFECTA

Jamie Boudreau, Canon, Seattle

Drawing on ingredients from countries where Romance languages are spoken, the Latin Trifecta honors Spain, Italy, and Mexico with the strong and savory trio of tequila, sherry, and Cynar. The effect is an intensely savory stirred cocktail that can act as a fortifying predinner drink or the evening's final salvo.

1 ounce tequila

1 ounce Cynar

½ ounce dry oloroso sherry

3 dashes orange bitters

Garnish flamed orange twist (see Note)

Combine the tequila, Cynar, sherry, and bitters in a mixing glass. Add ice, stir until chilled, and strain into a chilled coupe. Flame an orange twist, then drop the twist into the drink.

NOTE To flame an orange twist, take a thick piece of orange peel and angle its skin side just above the drink. Light a match and hold it in front of the peel, and squeeze to express its oils over the flame and the drink.

OAXACA OLD-FASHIONED

Phil Ward, New York

One of the most beloved modern-classic cocktails (both in bars across the country and at PUNCH), this play on the Old-Fashioned (page 39) swaps out whiskey for mezcal and a lightly aged tequila and sugar for agave syrup, placing it firmly within the rich-savory-smoky realm. The final layer of flavor comes by way of a flamed orange twist.

1½ ounces reposado tequila

½ ounce mezcal

2 dashes Angostura bitters

1 barspoon agave syrup

Garnish flamed orange twist (see Note)

Combine the tequila, mezcal, bitters, and agave in a rocks glass filled with one large ice cube. Stir until chilled. Flame an orange twist, then drop the twist into the drink.

NOTE To flame an orange twist, take a thick piece of orange peel and angle its skin side just above the drink. Light a match and hold it in front of the peel, and squeeze to express its oils over the flame and the drink.

CHUNKY CARDIGAN

Brad Thomas Parsons, Brooklyn

The Chunky Cardigan is a winterized reboot of Brad Thomas Parsons' Autumn Sweater, an amaro-rich seasonal drink that was one of the breakout cocktail recipes in his book *Bitters: A Spirited History of a Classic Cure-All.* This combination of the warm alpine herbs and spices delivered by Braulio with the natural smokiness from both Amaro Sfumato Rabarbaro and mezcal make for an aromatic cold-weather cocktail with a bright burst of wintertime citrus and floral honey sweetness.

1½ ounces Cappelletti Amaro Sfumato Rabarbaro

¾ ounce Amaro Braulio

¾ ounce mezcal

¾ ounce freshly squeezed grapefruit juice

½ ounce honey syrup (page 23)

2 pinches kosher salt

Garnish Scorched rosemary sprig (see Note), grapefruit twist

Combine the amari, mezcal, grapefruit juice, honey syrup, and salt in a cocktail shaker filled with ice. Shake until chilled and strain into a double rocks glass over a large ice cube. Garnish with the scorched rosemary and grapefruit twist.

NOTE To scorch the rosemary, gently char a fresh rosemary sprig with a kitchen torch, match, or open flame, carefully shaking the leaf to extinguish any lit flames or embers.

SEELBACH

Adam Seger, New York

At the turn of the twentieth century, a pair of Bavarian brothers, the Seelbachs, opened a posh hotel in downtown Louisville catering to upper-crust travelers. Its lavish interior evoked the Old World and attracted characters—like F. Scott Fitzgerald and Al Capone—who knew they could always get a stiff drink at the Seelbach Bar, even throughout Prohibition. The grand, saloon-style counter specialized in bourbon, and its signature cocktail was apparently created when a bartender used a Manhattan to catch the overflow from an uncorked champagne bottle. Or so the story went. The Seelbach's narrative has since been proven to be nothing more than a fabrication by the hotel's bartender, Adam Seger, in the 1990s, but the drink remains a staple nonetheless.

1 ounce bourbon
½ ounce Cointreau
7 dashes Angostura bitters
7 dashes Peychaud's bitters

Champagne or other dry sparkling wine, to top
Garnish orange twist

Combine the bourbon, Cointreau, and bitters in a mixing glass. Add ice, stir until chilled, and strain into a chilled flute or coupe. Top with champagne and garnish with an orange twist.

BLACK APPLE OLD-FASHIONED

Sother Teague, Amor y Amargo, New York

For most drinkers of a certain age, Jägermeister is the unofficial source of many a bad decision. But here it acts as the base of a bone-warming drink that combines the herbal notes of the liqueur with apple brandy for a decidedly adult way to fortify oneself after a day out in the cold.

1½ ounces Jägermeister

1 ounce apple brandy

2 dashes apple bitters

Garnish orange twist

Combine the Jägermeister, brandy, and bitters in an ice-filled rocks glass. Garnish with an orange twist.

EL DUQUE

Gabriel Orta and Elad Zvi, 27 Restaurant & Bar, Miami

From the classic template of the Manhattan (page 41), you can make an El Duque by substituting rum for bourbon and sherry for sweet vermouth. Then add a bit of cold-brew coffee and chocolate bitters for complexity, and you get a postprandial digestif meant to restart the night, rather than end it.

2 ounces aged rum

1 ounce cream sherry

½ ounce cold-brew coffee

3 dashes chocolate bitters

Garnish long, curly lemon twist

Combine the rum, sherry, coffee, and bitters in a mixing glass. Add ice, stir until chilled, and strain into a chilled cocktail glass. Garnish with a long, curly twist of lemon.

BOO RADLEY

Chris Hannah, French 75 Bar, New Orleans

Named after the mysterious neighbor in Harper Lee's great
Southern novel, *To Kill a Mockingbird*, the Boo Radley is a play
on another, more obscure Southern classic, the Creole cocktail.
Where the Creole uses rye whiskey, the Boo Radley substitutes
in bourbon, and in place of sweet vermouth there is Cynar, the
Italian artichoke amaro. Finally, instead of the esoteric bitter
orange liqueur Amer Picon, this calls on the godfather of cherry
brandies, Cherry Heering.

2 ounces bourbon	½ ounce Cherry Heering
¾ ounce Cynar	**Garnish** lemon and orange twists

Combine the bourbon, Cynar, and Cherry Heering in a mixing
glass. Add ice, stir until chilled, and strain into a chilled coupe.
Express a lemon twist and an orange twist over the cocktail
and drop the twists into the glass.

SUN STEALER

Henry Prendergast, Analogue, Chicago

One of our favorite winter cocktail ingredients, crème de cacao can give any drink a dessert-like kick in small doses. Here it's employed in a drink that started off as a martini-Manhattan love child but doubles down on the depth with the addition of crème de cacao's chocolate notes and the bitterness of Fernet-Branca. Think of it as the perfect dose of liquid courage before hitting the slopes.

2 ounces gin	¼ ounce Fernet-Branca
¾ ounce sweet vermouth	1 dash orange bitters
¼ ounce white crème de cacao	**Garnish** lemon twist

Combine the gin, vermouth, crème de cacao, Fernet-Branca, and bitters in a mixing glass. Add ice, stir, and strain into a coupe. Garnish with a lemon twist.

THE MEXICAN TRICYCLE

Andrew Volk, Portland Hunt & Alpine Club, Portland, Maine

The Mexican Tricycle was born as a cousin (twice removed) of the classic Italian aperitivo cocktail the Bicicletta, a combination Campari and white wine topped with soda water. Here, smoky mezcal acts as the backbone of the drink, standing up to the sweetness of the cider with an added kick of bitter Cynar—making for a simple, refreshing winter aperitif.

1 ounce mezcal, preferably Del Maguey Vida

1 ounce Cynar

Hard apple cider, preferably Bantam Wunderkind, to top

Garnish lime wheel

Combine the mezcal and Cynar in a tall collins glass. Fill with ice, top with cider, and garnish with a lime wheel.

OLD GRAMPIAN

Isaac Shumway, San Francisco

A mix of two scotches—one blended and one peated, from Islay—this riff on the old-fashioned originally appeared at the renewed iteration of San Francisco's Tosca Café. Where many old-fashioneds require a healthy stir, this one is meant to tell a story as the ice melts. Rich and complex with a touch of honey for sweetness and two kinds of bitters, this is a drink meant to be sipped slowly, and in good company.

1½ ounces blended scotch

½ ounce peated Islay scotch

1 barspoon rich honey syrup (see Note)

2 dashes Angostura bitters

1 dash orange bitters

Garnish orange twist

Combine the scotches, honey syrup, and bitters in a rocks glass. Squeeze the orange twist over the glass to express its oils and rub the peel around the inside of the glass. Set aside. Add a large piece of ice and stir briefly. Garnish with the orange twist.

NOTE To make rich honey syrup, follow the recipe for honey syrup (page 23), using 2 cups honey instead of 1 cup.

ACT OF FAITH

Dan Greenbaum, Diamond Reef, New York

On paper, the Act of Faith is a bit of an odd bird. A combination of two rich, funky rums and a whole ¼ ounce of Angostura bitters rounded out with a hit of sweet, raisiny Pedro Ximénez sherry, it builds on rich tropical flavors for a drink that still feels rooted farther north.

1½ ounces Jamaican rum

½ ounce blackstrap rum

½ ounce Pedro Ximénez sherry

¼ ounce Angostura bitters

Garnish orange twist

Pour the rums, sherry, and bitters into a rocks glass over a large ice cube and stir to chill. Garnish with an orange twist.

KING NEPTUNE'S TONIC

Karen Fu, New York

This low-alcohol, sherry-based winter spritz uses dark rum and coffee liqueur to prop up the savory, umami notes present in oloroso. It's then topped up with lightly bitter tonic water. Taken together, it's proof that a drink can be both complex and rich without being high octane.

1½ ounces dry oloroso sherry

¾ ounce dark rum

¾ ounce coffee liqueur, preferably Galliano Ristretto

½ ounce tonic water

Garnish grapefruit twist

Combine the sherry, rum, and coffee liqueur in a mixing glass. Add ice, stir to chill, and strain into a rocks glass over a large ice cube. Add the tonic water and garnish with a grapefruit twist.

CARROLL GARDENS

Joaquín Simó, Pouring Ribbons, New York

This contribution to the family of brown and stirred drinks named after New York neighborhoods nods to the Italian-American roots of Carroll Gardens. A base of American rye combined with an entirely Italian set of supporting ingredients creates a profile evocative of marzipan (hello, holiday cookies) and stone fruit.

2 ounces rye whiskey

½ ounce sweet vermouth

½ ounce Nardini amaro

1 scant teaspoon maraschino liqueur

Garnish lemon twist

Combine the whiskey, vermouth, amaro, and maraschino liqueur in a mixing glass. Add ice, stir until chilled, and strain into a chilled coupe. Express a lemon twist over the top and drop into the glass.

MEZCALETTI

Richard Boccato, Fresh Kills Bar, New York

The ingredients of the Mezcaletti are telegraphed in the name: mezcal and Amaro Meletti, built in a rocks glass over ice. The easygoing, bittersweet profile of Meletti alongside smoky, bracing mezcal has a surprising amount of depth for such a simple construction.

1 ounce mezcal	2 dashes orange bitters
1 ounce Amaro Meletti	**Garnish** lemon twist

Pour the mezcal, Meletti, and bitters into a rocks glass over a large ice cube. Gently stir ten to fifteen times. Express a lemon twist over the top and drop into the glass.

IMPROVED HOT TODDY

Editors of PUNCH, New York

What do you do when you desperately need a hot toddy and the lemons in your fridge are at least a month old? One winter, instead of walking in the cold to re-up, we grabbed a bottle of Bragg Apple Cider Vinegar—the answer to all that ails—and used it as a replacement. Our official variation calls for it in addition to fresh lemon juice.

2 ounces bourbon

1 ounce freshly squeezed lemon juice

¾ ounce pure maple syrup

¾ ounce apple cider vinegar, preferably Bragg

Hot water, to top

Garnish lemon wheel, cinnamon stick, and star anise pod

Combine the bourbon, lemon juice, maple syrup, and cider vinegar in a tempered mug. Add hot water and stir until the syrup is dissolved. Garnish with a lemon wheel, cinnamon stick, and star anise pod.

IRISH COFFEE

The Dead Rabbit Grocery & Grog, New York

Making a great hot drink has a lot to do with temperature. In the case of the Dead Rabbit's famous Irish Coffee, the correct temperature—right around 75°F—prevents the coffee from taking on a burnt, metallic taste. Another key component to this Irish-American classic is the glassware: a tempered glass will stand up to heat, and also showcases the drink's layers of dark coffee, whiskey, and sugar beneath very soft, barely whipped heavy cream.

1½ ounces Irish whiskey, preferably Powers Gold Label

4 ounces hot filtered coffee

½ ounce demerara syrup (see Note)

1 ounce whipped heavy cream (see Note)

Garnish freshly grated nutmeg

Pour the whiskey, coffee, and demerara syrup into an Irish coffee glass. Float an inch of whipped cream on top. Garnish with freshly grated nutmeg.

NOTE To whip cream, place a metal bowl and whisk in the freezer for 10 to 15 minutes to chill. Remove, pour in a cup of heavy cream, and whip until it begins to thicken, 1 to 2 minutes. Be careful not to overbeat; the consistency should still be loose enough to spoon over the top of the drink.

To make demerara syrup, follow the recipe for simple syrup (page 23), substituting rich demerara sugar for regular cane sugar.

ONE HOT GINGER

Simone Goldberg, The Standard Hotel, East Village, New York

This blend of bourbon, Grand Marnier, cayenne pepper, and ginger mashes up the hot toddy with a classic juice bar cold remedy for a double-duty winter drink.

4½ ounces hot water

1½ ounces bourbon

1 ounce freshly squeezed lemon juice

1 ounce ginger syrup (page 22)

¾ ounce Grand Marnier

2 dashes Angostura bitters

Pinch of cayenne pepper

Garnish orange twist

Pour the hot water, bourbon, lemon juice, ginger syrup, Grand Marnier, and bitters into a tempered mug. Add the cayenne and stir. Express an orange twist over the glass and drop into the glass.

PEPPERMINT BARK EGGNOG

Tom Macy, Clover Club, New York

This single-serve riff on classic eggnog blends two essential cool-weather flavors—chocolate and mint—with both rum and cognac for a cocktail that drinks like a boozy take on mint chocolate chip ice cream.

1 ounce aged rum

1 ounce cognac, preferably V.S. or V.S.O.P.

½ ounce white crème de menthe

½ ounce white crème de cacao

½ ounce heavy cream

1 whole egg

Garnish freshly grated nutmeg and finely crushed peppermint bark or peppermint candy (optional)

Combine the rum, cognac, crème de menthe, crème de cacao, cream, and egg in a a cocktail shaker. Add ice, shake until chilled, and strain into a coupe. Garnish with grated nutmeg and peppermint bark dust.

MULLED WINE

Editors of PUNCH, New York

Mulled wine is the sort of quintessential winter drink that can, in one simmering pot, embody the holiday season. It's a drink that goes by many names (*glögg* in Sweden, *vin chaud* in France, *Glühwein* in Germany) and is the subject of countless iterations. We consider ours to be a baseline mulled wine—packed with all of the requisite baking spices, but also meant to be built upon if you so desire. **SERVES 8 TO 10**

1 (750 ml) bottle full-bodied, unoaked red wine

1½ cups brandy

1 cup sweet vermouth, preferably Miro Rojo

1 teaspoon freshly grated ginger

20 whole cloves

5 allspice berries

4 cinnamon sticks, broken up

3 star anise pods

Zest of 1 orange

½ to ¾ cup sugar

Garnish 8 to 10 clove-studded orange half-wheels and cinnamon sticks

Combine the wine, brandy, vermouth, ginger, cloves, allspice, cinnamon, star anise, and orange zest and heat in a saucepan over medium heat, taking care to not let it boil. Once hot, add ½ cup sugar and stir until dissolved; for additional sweetness, add an additional ¼ cup sugar. Reduce heat to low and let steep for 30 minutes. Strain, ladle into individual cups, and garnish with the clove-studded orange half-wheel and a cinnamon stick.

DANGER ZONE

Alla Lapushchik, OTB, New York

The Danger Zone mixes rum, nutty Frangelico, citrus, and a whole egg in a tall flip that drinks like the love child of eggnog and an Orange Julius.

1½ ounces Venezuelan rum, preferably Santa Teresa 1796

¾ ounce Frangelico

¾ ounce freshly squeezed orange juice

½ ounce freshly squeezed lemon juice

½ ounce simple syrup (page 23)

1 whole egg

Soda water, to top

Garnish 2 dashes Angostura bitters

Combine the rum, Frangelico, orange juice, lemon juice, simple syrup, and egg in a cocktail shaker. Dry shake (shake without ice). Add ice and shake until chilled. Strain into a tall collins glass and top with soda water. Garnish with two dashes of Angostura.

BRANDY ZANDER

Editors of PUNCH, New York

The Brandy Zander is our riff on the classic brandy Alexander, also known as the Alexander no. 2, a classic mix of equal parts brandy, crème de cacao, and cream dusted with freshly grated nutmeg. While one of the earliest known mentions of the drink (featuring gin) is attributed to Hugo Ensslin's 1917 *Recipes for Mixed Drinks,* the drink reached its height during America's disco days. Our recipe ups the measure of brandy (we recommend cognac) and adds a bonus dose of cold-brew coffee, which helps dry out the drink and give it an extra layer of depth.

2 ounces cognac

1 ounce crème de cacao

1 ounce heavy cream

½ ounce cold-brew coffee

Garnish freshly grated nutmeg

Pour the cognac, crème de cacao, cream, and coffee into a cocktail shaker. Add ice, shake until chilled, and strain into a coupe. Garnish with nutmeg.

PIÑA COLADA
MILK PUNCH

Editors of PUNCH, New York

The piña colada so singularly symbolizes summer, it seems an almost impossible feat to make it winter appropriate. *Almost.* This punch maintains the drink's tropical essence, but transforms it by adding comforting scalded milk. **SERVES 8**

14 ounces aged rum

8 ounces coconut water

4 ounces Velvet falernum

4 ounces pineapple juice

3 ounces freshly squeezed lime juice

1 ounce demerara syrup (see Note)

6 ounces whole milk

Garnish freshly grated nutmeg

Pour the rum, coconut water, Velvet falernum, pineapple juice, lime juice, and demerara syrup into a heatsafe mixing bowl. Over medium-low heat, heat the milk in a saucepan, stirring continuously until the milk begins to bubble around the edges (taking care not to let it boil). Add the milk to the mixing bowl, stir until it begins to coagulate, and let the mixture sit for 15 minutes. Strain through a cheesecloth or coffee filter until the mixture is clarified. Ladle into cups over ice and garnish with grated nutmeg.

NOTE To make demerara syrup, follow the recipe for simple syrup (page 23), substituting rich demerara sugar for regular cane sugar.

DO NOT GO GENTLE INTO THAT GOOD NIGHT

Chantal Tseng, Reading Room, Washington, DC

This drink is proof that you can give your hot toddy an avant-garde turn without too much extra work. Here, a combination of bergamot-accented Earl Grey and smoky scotch commingles with the X-factor addition of allspice dram, which offers a bear-hug of warm spice notes in one small dose.

4 ounces hot Earl Grey tea

1½ ounces peated blended scotch

½ ounce honey syrup (page 23)

¼ ounce St. Elizabeth Allspice Dram

¼ ounce freshly squeezed lemon juice

Garnish scorched star anise pod (see Note)

Combine the tea, scotch, honey syrup, allspice dram, and lemon juice in a clear tempered mug and stir gently to combine. Garnish with a scorched star anise pod.

NOTE To scorch the star anise, gently char a star anise pod with a kitchen torch, match, or open flame.

SPIKED HORCHATA

Editors of PUNCH, New York

Our boozy ode to the cinnamon-infused Mexican almond and rice milk beverage simplifies the ingredients and build. To a homemade horchata (which includes pecans for extra richness), we add bourbon and a hit of (optional) cold-brew coffee, all served over ice with a generous dusting of grated cinnamon. Word of advice: consider doubling the horchata recipe to reserve some for booze-free day drinking.

3 ounces horchata (recipe opposite)

1½ ounces aged rum

½ ounce cold-brew coffee (optional)

Garnish grated cinnamon

Combine the horchata, rum, and coffee over ice in a rocks glass and stir to chill. Garnish with grated cinnamon.

HORCHATA

1 cup short-grain white rice

1 cup almonds

1 cup pecans

3 cups water

1 cup almond milk

½ cup agave syrup

1 teaspoon ground cinnamon

1 teaspoon vanilla extract

Combine the rice, almonds, and pecans in a blender and blend until pulverized. Add the water, almond milk, agave, cinnamon, and vanilla and blend to combine (you may need to work in batches, depending on your blender's capacity). Transfer to a large container and refrigerate overnight. Strain through cheesecloth, bottle, and refrigerate for up to a week. **MAKES 4 CUPS**

WEEKNIGHT WASSAIL

Editors of PUNCH, New York

The word *wassail* has been used for more than a thousand years, appearing as early as the eighth century in the poem "Beowulf." Throughout the single-digit centuries, it was used as either a salutation (wassail!) or an adjective (get wassailed). It was first applied to a steaming bowl of ale and fortified wine around the thirteenth century and the "wassail bowl" evolved to become an offering of peace and prosperity during the holidays. Our version simplifies the sometimes labor-intensive hot drink to make it a candidate for casual weeknight winter drinking. **SERVES 10**

4 cups fresh-pressed apple cider

2 cups apple brandy

2 cups oloroso sherry

¼ cup brown sugar

20 whole cloves

10 allspice berries

4 cinnamon sticks

2-inch piece ginger, peeled and sliced

Garnish 10 cinnamon sticks (optional) and 10 apple slices

Combine the cider, brandy, sherry, brown sugar, cloves, allspice, cinnamon, and ginger in a large saucepan over low heat. Simmer over very low heat, stirring occasionally, for 20 minutes. Strain the mixture and pour into tempered mugs. Garnish each mug with an apple slice and cinnamon stick.

BARBARY COAST

William Elliott, Maison Premiere, New York

On paper this drink is sure to raise a few eyebrows. Break it down to each of its ingredients, though, and it channels many of the flavors we associate with winter drinking: smoke, chocolate, herbs, spice, and cream. Think of it as a more complex sub-in for eggnog.

1 ounce crème de cacao, preferably Tempus Fugit Spirits

1 ounce gin

1 ounce peated Islay scotch

1 ounce heavy cream

6 drops rose water (optional)

3 dashes Angostura bitters

Garnish orange twist, freshly grated nutmeg

Combine the crème de cacao, gin, scotch, cream, rose water, and bitters in a cocktail shaker. Add ice, shake, and strain into a Nick & Nora glass or a coupe. Express an orange twist over the glass and discard. Top with grated nutmeg.

NOTE While the addition of rose water takes this drink to the next level, it's still plenty delicious without it.

AVERNA STOUT FLIP

Jacob Grier, Portland, Oregon

Beer cocktail guru Jacob Grier, author of *Cocktails on Tap*, calls the Averna Stout Flip one of his favorite creations. Working with the idea that dark beer likes dark spirits, this boozy milkshake-like concoction works best with heavier stouts, like Young's Double Chocolate Stout or Samuel Smith's Oatmeal Stout.

1 large egg	2 dashes Angostura bitters
2 ounces Amaro Averna	**Garnish** freshly grated nutmeg
1 ounce stout	

Crack the egg into a shaker and add the Averna, stout, bitters, and ice. Shake hard until cold and frothy and strain into a wineglass. Garnish with freshly grated nutmeg.

JALISCO HOT CHOCOLATE

Editors of PUNCH, New York

A match ordained by the gods, this Mexican hot chocolate (your standard-issue hot chocolate upgraded with cinnamon and chile pepper) spiked with tequila is the very definition of a winter cocktail: transporting, fortifying, and still gluggable. **SERVES 4**

3 cups whole milk

¾ cup semisweet chocolate chips

1 tablespoon brown sugar

⅛ teaspoon cayenne pepper

⅛ teaspoon ancho chile powder

½ teaspoon ground cinnamon

½ teaspoon vanilla extract

1 cup blanco tequila

Garnish 4 cinnamon sticks or 4 whole dried ancho chiles

Combine the milk, chocolate chips, brown sugar, cayenne, chile powder, cinnamon, and vanilla in a saucepan over medium heat, whisking continually until the chocolate is dissolved, about 7 minutes. Divide the tequila among four mugs (2 ounces in each) and pour the hot chocolate mix into each. Garnish each mug with a cinnamon stick or whole dried ancho chile.

FRENCH TOAST FLIP

Erick Castro, Polite Provisions, San Diego

This riff on the classic sherry flip (sherry, sugar, and a whole egg shaken into submission) ups the ante with scotch and apple brandy. And it's true to its name, perfectly channeling the rich, comforting smack of maple syrup-covered French toast.

1 ounce oloroso sherry

¾ ounce scotch

¾ ounce Laird's Applejack or Apple Brandy 100

4 ounces pure maple syrup

1 whole egg

2 dashes whiskey barrel–aged bitters, preferably Fee Brothers

Garnish freshly grated cinnamon

Combine the sherry, scotch, applejack, maple syrup, egg, and bitters in a cocktail shaker and dry shake (shake without ice). Add ice, shake vigorously until chilled, and strain into a small mug or sour glass. Garnish with freshly grated cinnamon.

À LA MODE

Karin Stanley, Dutch Kills, New York

This combination of fresh apple cider, bourbon, and Licor 43
(a citrus and vanilla–tinged Spanish liqueur) is meant to channel
the flavor of apple pie *à la mode*. But this spiced, creamy ode
to the American classic is almost better than the thing itself.
Because, well, bourbon.

4 ounces heavy cream	1 ounce bourbon
1 cube or barspoon brown sugar	½ ounce Licor 43
5 ounces fresh-pressed apple cider	**Garnish** freshly grated nutmeg

Combine the cream and brown sugar cube in a cocktail shaker.
Add the coil of a Hawthorne strainer and dry shake (shake
without ice) to aerate but not whip into stiffness. It must be
lightened but still pourable. In a saucepan, heat the apple cider,
bourbon, and Licor 43 over low heat until steaming, about
10 minutes. Pour into a tempered mug and carefully top the
drink with a finger of whipped cream. Garnish with freshly
grated nutmeg.

CHARTREUSE TODDY

The Editors of PUNCH, New York

While workshopping riffs on the classic hot toddy, we wanted to create something that played close enough to the original tune, but felt a bit more tony, more deluxe, more *French*. This combination of cognac (French) and the herbal liqueur Chartreuse (French) plus the usual toddy trappings, is the perfect amount of French.

1½ ounces cognac

¾ ounce green Chartreuse

½ ounce freshly squeezed lemon juice

½ ounce honey syrup (page 23)

Garnish star anise pod

Combine the cognac, Chartreuse, lemon juice, and honey syrup in a clear tempered mug and garnish with a star anise pod.

AMARO CALDO

Joe Campanale, Fausto, Brooklyn

Our good friend the Brooklyn restaurateur and sommelier Joe Campanale first had this warming combination of steaming hot water and amaro with a group of boar hunters in the Tuscan town of Panzano. It's about as easy as it gets and reinforces our view that amaro is its own bottled cocktail—just add water.

4 ounces hot water

2 ounces amaro

Garnish lemon twist

Combine the hot water with your favorite amaro in a tempered glass. Express a lemon twist over the top and drop it into the glass.

CHAI MILK PUNCH

Brian Bartels, Happy Cooking Hospitality, New York

This dairy-free milk punch channels winter drinking in the 1990s, when Starbucks first turned the chai latte into a global phenomenon. Here it gets a double dose of holiday-forward spice from cinnamon syrup and a dusting of fresh nutmeg.

4 ounces chai-infused vanilla almond milk (see Note)

1½ ounces bourbon

½ ounce cinnamon syrup (page 21)

Garnish freshly grated nutmeg

Combine the almond milk, bourbon, and cinnamon syrup in a cocktail shaker. Add ice, shake, and strain over ice into a double rocks glass. Garnish with freshly grated nutmeg.

NOTE To make chai-infused vanilla almond milk, pour 10 ounces of sweetened vanilla almond milk into a saucepan over medium-low heat. Add 1 chai tea bag and allow it to steep for 15 minutes, making sure that the mixture does not come to a boil. Remove the pan from the heat and let the mixture cool before removing the chai bag. Refrigerate.

HOT DAIQUIRI

Kathleen Hawkins, Wright and Company, Detroit

While turning a summer drink like the daiquiri into what is essentially a rum hot toddy seems like a bibulous fool's errand, this drink is something of a nonsensical triumph. And it is one hell of a holiday party trick.

3 ounces hot water

1 ounce dark rum, preferably Diplomatico Reserva Exclusiva

1 ounce Plantation Pineapple Rum

½ ounce simple syrup (page 23)

½ ounce freshly squeezed lime juice

Angostura whipped cream, to top (see Note)

Combine the hot water, dark rum, pineapple rum, simple syrup, and lime juice in a tempered glass or mug and top with 2 to 3 tablespoons whipped cream.

NOTE To make Angostura whipped cream, add 16 dashes of Angsotura bitters to 1 cup heavy cream. Whip by hand in a chilled metal bowl until stiff, about 2 minutes.

ARMADA PUNCH

Editors of PUNCH, New York

It's true that escapism is most commonly associated with drinks of the tropical persuasion. But no one ever said that a winter drink can't do the same. Think of this combination of Guatemalan rum, citrus, and spice as your postcard from summer. **SERVES 8**

2 Earl Grey tea bags

1½ cups aged rum, preferably Ron Zacapa 23 Sistema Solera

1½ cups ounces oloroso sherry

½ cup lemon juice

½ cup lime juice

1 cup cinnamon syrup (page 21)

1 teaspoon Angostura bitters

Garnish star anise pods, orange half wheels, grated nutmeg

Boil 2 cups water and steep the tea bags in it for 3 minutes. Set aside to cool. In a punch bowl, combine the rum, sherry, lemon and lime juices, bitters, and cinnamon syrup. Stir to mix. Add the tea. If serving immediately, add several large cubes of ice to the punch bowl, along with orange wheels and star anise pods. Ladle into punch cups over ice and garnish with grated nutmeg.

NOTE To serve the punch warm, boil 2 cups water in a saucepan. Turn off the heat, add the tea bags, and steep for 3 minutes. Remove the tea bags, add the rum, sherry, lemon and lime juices, cinnamon syrup, bitters, star anise pods, and orange wheels. Stir to combine, then warm slowly over low heat. Ladle into punch cups and garnish with grated nutmeg.

ACKNOWLEDGMENTS

Thank you, firstly, to all of the bartenders who have graciously allowed us to feature their recipes on PUNCH and inspired our own drink-making in these pages. Audrey Sanders, Erik Adkins, Jamie Boudreau, Leo Robitschek, Damon Boelte, Sam Ross, Dan Sabo, Ryan Fitzgerald, Natasha David, Brad Ferran, Lucinda Sterling, the staff at Diamond Reef, Jason Kosmas, Jon Santer, Phil Ward, Brad Thomas Parsons, Adam Seger, Sother Teague, Gabriel Orta, Elad Zvi, Chris Hannah, Henry Pendergast, Andrew Volk, Isaac Shumway, Dan Greenbaum, Karen Fu, Joaquín Simó, Richard Boccato, Simone Goldberg, the staff at the Dead Rabbit, Tom Macy, Alla Lapushchik, Chantal Tseng, William Elliott, Jacob Grier, Erick Castro, Karin Stanley, Joe Campanale, Brian Bartels, Kathleen Hawkins, this is for all of you.

Thank you to Julie Bennett and Anne Goldberg from Ten Speed Press for shepherding this project along with grace, kindness, and patience. To Margaux Keres, the book's designer and prop stylist, for schlepping across the country and between dozens of Ubers to make this happen. To Emma Campion for her guidance and savvy, always. To the entire production team at Ten Speed Press. To Ricky Agustin for being the biggest badass there ever was and for styling all of the drinks for every shoot like a pro—and, more importantly, for having the best attitude in the room while doing it (and it wasn't always easy). To the teams at Rider, Freemans, and Faun for letting us invade your beautiful restaurants and make complete messes of them. We owe you times infinity.

And, lastly, thank you to winter for inspiring us to fortify ourselves against you. This is for you, too.

INDEX

Published in the United States by Ten Speed Press, an imprint of
the Crown Publishing Group, a division of Penguin Random House
LLC, New York.
www.crownpublishing.com
www.tenspeed.com
punchdrink.com

Ten Speed Press and the Ten Speed Press colophon are registered
trademarks of Penguin Random House LLC.

Library of Congress Cataloging-in-Publication Data
Names: Ten Speed Press
Title: Winter drinks : 70 essential cold-weather cocktails / editors of
    PUNCH.
Other titles: Punch (Berkeley, Calif.)
Description: First edition. | California : Ten Speed Press, [2018] |
    Includes index.
Identifiers: LCCN 2018006298
Subjects: LCSH: Cocktails. | LCGFT: Cookbooks
Classification: LCC TX951 .W538 2018 | DDC 641.87/4—dc23
LC record available at https://lccn.loc.gov/2018006298

Hardcover ISBN: 978-0-399-58166-3
eBook ISBN: 978-0-399-58167-0

Printed in China

Design and prop styling by Margaux Keres
Drink styling by Rickey Agustin

10 9 8 7 6 5 4 3 2 1

First Edition